HARDPRESS.NET
HOME OF HARD-TO-FIND BOOKS

Notabilities in France and England
by Philarète Chasles

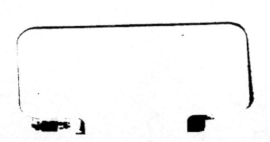

NOTABILITIES

IN

FRANCE AND ENGLAND.

NOTABILITIES

IN

FRANCE AND ENGLAND.

With an Autobiography.

BY

PHILARETE CHASLES,

PROFESSOR OF THE PARIS INSTITUTE.

New York:

G. P. PUTNAM & CO., 10 PARK PLACE.

M.DCCC.LIII.

Preface by the Translator.

WITHOUT any display, the writer of these sketches reveals much of his early life, and he is very frank in speaking of his own country. From his long exile he returned almost an Englishman in his views of morals and politics. He was subject to none of the illusions to which his native country is so prone, and did not dream of perfectibility by shaking off the fetters of monarchy. But he will reveal his views in his own words.

The title of the work from which I have translated the following pages is, "Studies upon Men and Manners of the Nineteenth Century." It consists of recollections of youth, contemporary portraits, sketches of travel, and thoughts upon France. The writer is a Professor at the Paris Institute. It is reported that he is coming to this country to lecture ; in that case our interest to know something of him from his works is increased. His stories interested me from the novelty and vividness of his description ; and his observations, from their strong good sense and glow of moral feeling. His representations of the state of society in his own country concur with some other writers of his own nation.

I have translated his prison life entire,—also his stories; his thoughts upon France, which might take the form of essays, fill the limited space that remains; but I have selected, I think, the most striking of his remarks. The undying interest which is manifested for France, continually brings to light new incidents from revolutionary times, from those of Bonaparte's despotism, and the present tyrannical rule of the ignoble and dastardly usurper. Anecdotes of French saloons, French dungeons, politics, literature &c., abound, and find untiring readers; which leads me to hope that the translations from this author will not be unacceptable.

Preface by the Author.

————•————

THESE modest studies upon the men and manners of my time form the natural complement to the twelve volumes which preceded.* Intermingled as these memorials are with scenes in the writer's life, they are far from pretending to the title of memoirs or personal biography. If the author appears sometimes too prominent, it is neither his fault nor desire; but in speaking of facts and of men, it was necessary to explain from what point he viewed them, and the modifications that his literary ideas have received from his experience and the events of life. In admiring contemporary talents he followed no school, bowed before no idol; this was the inevitable consequence of a youth cast on desolate shores, and removed from the ordinary routine.

To sketches of travels in the interior of England and Ireland succeed some critical observations, very severe,

———————————————————————————————

* The volumes referred to are, "Studies upon the most Prominent European Nations of Various Ages,"—as the Middle age,—the age of Louis the 14th,—Cromwell's time,—they form the complement of his works, but cannot be necessarily connected with this.

upon the doctrines of the times in which I lived, and upon the influence they have exercised upon the people. These appeared the first time in parts, till they offended a people carried away by the material, and proceeding to the abyss which had been pointed out to them in vain ; since then I collected and entitled them Historical Documents, not lessons or warnings—still less a satire, general or personal, which would not at this day require courage, and would fail in dignity. Added to these criticisms, or strictures, are descriptions of some singular characters whom I have known, and who have disappeared from the agitated scene of which we are spectators ; among foreigners are Coleridge, Foscolo, Bentham ;—French, M. de Chateaubriand ;—with two who played a peculiar part in our revolutionary assembly, Vadier and Amar.

Whatever may be the severity of the strictures upon certain points in morals and religion which these pages contain, it would be an error to believe that the writer would claim the title of austere moralist and the honours of superior virtue. Right or wrong, the question is between God and himself ; sincere, ardent, frequently sad, he sincerely loves the true and good ; those who have lived between 1815 and 1840 cannot be astonished at the grief which filled his heart when he returned to France that he quitted at a very early age. He then found his country more miserable and agitated than ever. By his good or ill fortune, he was, for the first years after his return to France, condemned to a perfect isolation in the midst of French society, for he could side with no party ; and this impartiality subjected him to more suffering than others, as he saw much to censure in his beloved country. Originality belongs then to the situation, and not to the writer; his grief was not the melancholy of caprice, but inevitable from the peculiarity of his situation.

The papers upon France were addressed to friends of the writer; to those who placed trust in the sincerity of a studious man and an observer. They perceived that any singularity of thought or style, for which he received praise or censure, proceeded not from eccentricity, or from the peevishness and discontent of an office-hunter, but from the strangeness of events. They cannot suspect him of any romantic claims, or affected severity towards his contemporaries; and now that his previsions are realized, his opinions can produce no surprise. The solitary recluse needs little effort to see justly; his view is not disturbed by the turmoil and confusion of party.

Some of these fragmentary pieces date from the distant period of my residence in London, where I occupied a small apartment in the vicinity of Hyde Park and Grosvenor Square. I was between fourteen and fifteen when the anathemas of Byron flashed upon us from Italy; I was in London when the enchanting fictions of Walter Scott were first published. O, how I luxuriated with these two geniuses in the garden of the Queen, by the serpentine stream. The first balls I attended were those of Grosvenor Square; and the ardent Platonism which at that time took a deep hold of my being may be traced in these studies. Happy he who lives in the inner life! What a charm in introver-

1*

sion,—to descend into the depths of one's being; to
usher before the tribunal within books and their critics,
schools and their disciples, restorations and revolutions,
memoirs and histories, reactions and glories! With
what power the passions, compressed in youth, recompensed me by energy and activity for what had failed
me in vain pleasures! Above all, I rejoiced in the self-
dependence I gained; I learned from that time to contemn the renown of authorship! Our intellectual gifts
are imparted to us to elevate us above such vanities.
The light of the spirit, kindled at the supreme source,
which is God himself, was not given for light purposes.
Religious reflection and independence of the praise of
man brings calmness in the present and tranquillity in
our view of the future; in action, we are temperate;
in writing, willing to abide our time, and seek not for
favour. By uniting with the diseased of the nation in
their periodical fury, or sharing with the insensate
masses, either as Chartes constitutionalists or worshippers of despotism, we pretend not to be more wise;
but, alas! who is wise? By this independent course a
person is better prepared to write the history of his
times, and to instruct future generations from the lessons
of the past; thereby we retain our love for truth, which
consoles us almost under the absence of every other
good. The ardent love of truth has taken possession
of my spirit since the sad period of my youth.

Thanks to her, it may be granted to me at a future
day to bequeath to posterity some traces, some living
and exact memorials, of the society so given to reaction,
so painfully fluctuating before my eyes,—of her strange

phases, her puffing and parading, her dwarfs who call themselves great, of her valets who style themselves masters, and of her recognised grandeur and virtues.

PHILARETE CHASLES.

INSTITUTE, 15*th December*, 1849.

CONTENTS.

Autobiography.

EARLY LIFE.

IT is not the greatness of a man that renders his memoirs interesting ; neither is it his heroism, his rank, nor even his romantic adventures, which enchain our attention, but it is the power of truth. Truth is the basis of the arts ; and even of poetry herself, which is thought to live by fiction. If there is cause to suspect vagueness or reservation in a man's confidences, we turn away with disgust.

The moving scene of which I was the youthful witness, impels me to write. I would not dispose the flambeaux so as in my own person to create an optical illusion ; such displays of vanity inspire me with pity. I speak of my own impressions that I may the better reproduce the actors in the scene ; for emotion is the most lively part of observation : I would be true to fact and feeling.

My earliest infantile recollections, which will always remain engraven on my heart, are of a sad and peculiar cast. I recall to mind a square and dark chamber, with closed shutters, the bell muffled with cotton, the persons within walking upon tiptoe, speaking in whispers, who watched the door with fear, and cautiously and slowly half opened the shutter to look out, and flitted like shadows round my bed. Here was I cradled, and here was the scene of my childhood. A heavy cloud overshadowed my infancy, and has hovered over me through life, which I date from this era; the recollection of it is as of yesterday. The twilight of the chamber always has remained, even in my moments of joy and success. A little serinette which aroused the child from his slumbers, but not to daylight, brought the mother to his cradle at the foot of her bed ; and her presence was as a gleam of sunshine. Youthful, lovely, blooming, methinks I still see her smile, which always beamed upon me ; still the same, even when enduring sorrow and anguish from her acute sensibility. At twenty-one years of age she married my father, a man of fifty-five, proscribed and crippled. Age had not diminished his ardour of head, heart, or temperament. He was a representative of that burning fiery zeal peculiar to the eighteenth century. It was the fever of the blood—the ceaseless roar of thunder—a water-spout in place of a breeze, to swell the sail. Our age has no idea of such spirits as then were upon the scenes : the Abbé Raynal, Diderot, Mirabeau, and others. Pity, charity, and generous sentiments, were natural to my father ; the habit of conspiring and declaiming was the life of his life, as with Mably.

It was then the commencement of the empire. Bonaparte would only suffer *Talma* to declaim ; to conspire and meddle with his artillery, no one. There rests the explanation of our closed room, and the tomb of my birth. My father lived secluded in this little study, reading Rousseau, as I have been told, for he was sincere in his admiration of him. My mother, apparently bright and happy, wept when alone ; she would always give me the morning embrace, for the little bird-organ was faithful to its duty.

At that time proscription was no joke ; the political game, in which one risks very little in 1846, had then for stake the heads of the players. My father had taken a very active part in the last efforts of the Republic, and he had returned without permission to conceal himself in Paris, with a young wife, (my mother,) and her eldest son, (myself,) whom he had named Philarète. I acknowledge, though I venerate the sincerity of my father, I do not share his dogmas. I have none of the enthusiasm of the eighteenth century, and that ardour for the anti-Christian crusade which it embraced.

The third story of the retreat which so sadly sheltered my father and my infancy, was owned by the uncle of the psychologist, the most subtile and refined of our age—M. Sainte-Beuve. It has now been taken down. It stood in the centre of the old city, and was designed for a parliamentary building; it bore a solemn and citizen-like majesty. My father being comprehended in the general amnesty which extended the imperial mantle over political offenders, then removed from the Isle of the city; to tell the truth, he had placed himself there as in a centre, where the proscribed could easily elude the governmental bloodhounds. Then he purchased a house, (Rue de Postes,) solitary, with a large garden, a terrace, a lawn, and grove of lofty trees, with a wall and a large gate

to secure the enclosures. And there he immured himself
with his anger, a large dog, and his Deistical library, which
contained more than a thousand volumes against Christianity;
and this last was my education. Bonaparte in the mean
time occupied himself with the training of Europe, and he
reaped his reward in kind.

All the waifs of the Republic, all the spared heads, or those
only slightly chafed by the great tempest, gathered round my
father; but his companions visited him as by stealth, feeling
their way along, lest they should be entrapped.

By a singular coincidence of circumstances, in the new
house which my father had purchased, there dwelt the father
of my contemporary, that very ingenious novelist, M. Mèrimèe,
who was there educated. At this time it is inhabited by
M. Michelet.——There is a destiny for houses as for books.

Thus the broken rigging, the fragments and wrecks of the
ship of the Republic rolled along by the waves, stranded upon
the beach, and covered with foam, were heaped at the feet of
a child. Then this child saw face to face the thundering
Titans ; after this he lived with the friends of Byron in London ; then with those who overthrew absolute monarchy in
Paris ; and, in fine, with the enemies of the last. To my infantile eyes the Titans of the Revolution seemed only men. I
surveyed these historical giants with the keen, scrutinizing
eyes of a child ; they seemed to me neither so ferocious nor
so sanguinary and terrible as I had been told they were. I
soon then began to distrust appearances, and even history ;
I began to observe minutely, and to look below, within, and

behind the scenes. When later I read in memoirs that the ferocious Amar was a wolf, that Mallarme had presided over the most terrible scenes of the Convention, and that Vadier was a hyena, I did not hearken to it. These wolves and hyenas were very good people, and I painted them such as my childhood had seen them, without partiality. Youth sees justly, and grants no pardons. Childhood, above all, is severe. La Fontaine knew it well.

All these men were neither good nor bad in themselves, but they abhorred and spoke ill of each other. A. censured B., who amused himself with C., and C. laughed secretly at D., who spared not E.; E. related good stories of F., which I repeated as apropos to G., H., and I. An intense passion carried each one along, as a torrent the swimmer, lifting him to the top of the waters, as it impels his course. They appeared great and redoubtable as they bounded over the sanguinary and tumultuous floods of the Revolution. Out of the impetuous current, and with some few exceptions, they were the most innocent people in the world ; characters feeble, otherwise they would have perished ; ardent, or they would not have been lifted to the summit of the revolutionary billows ; false in their views of themselves, not to perceive that this upheaving of society was not their work, or work for them to engage in ; in fine, mediocre, for the most part, as to intelligence, but not cruel.

Among the revolutionists whom I scanned in my early days, there were three species, the Archæists, imitators of antiquity —these proceeded from Jean Jacques ; the Sceptical, progeny

of Voltaire ; and, last, the Mystics, the most to be feared of
all, but they were rare ; it might be that they had chosen as
guide Swedenborg, Weisshaupt, Pascal, or Jacob Boehme.
The Voltairians, in their new organization of the Republic,
retained many of the ideas, habits, and customs of the monarchy ; with the sincere Archæists, the revival of antiquity
was a firm belief—the Rome of Brutus was to be resuscitated;
as to the Mystics, they accused themselves of only one crime,
that of not purchasing the Revolution by more blood. I will
endeavour to sketch one or two of these singular men.

VADIER, THE VOLTAIRIAN.

The king of the Voltairian Conventionals was Vadier.   Picture to yourself Voltaire at eighty years of age, his nose hooked,
his chin sharp, his eye twinkling in its orbit, and his figure
reduced to the anatomy of a man; moreover, imagine him a
Gascon, wooing in courtly strains with the vivacious playful-
ness of the Provençal.   There you have Vadier!   Like his prototype, there was a point of interrogation in every phrase—an
epigram in each smile—malice in each posture.   He was tall,
like Saturn,* withered, parched, and bony as he ; a few stray
white hairs were scattered here and there, and dangling over
his otherwise bald head ; his hooked nose and pointed chin
nearly met, and each feature and bone in his figure was angular.
Near him, and almost always standing, was a tall and beau-

---

* Voltaire.

tiful brunette, whose tint and expression marked her as a Provençale ; her eyes were remarkable, for they were at the same time ardent and fixed, and beneath a bright exterior you saw in the depths a deep melancholy ; this astonished the child as an irreconcilable union. Nothing was more curious also than to meet in the apartment of the monosyllabic Vadier some revolutionary adept of Jean Jacques and of Raynal, ardent and glowing, more eloquent even in his silence and gestures than in his rare discourse ; it was the snow in the neighbourhood of the volcano.

The aspect of Vadier defied my infant scrutiny, and affected me as something mysterious, though the bold destroyers of the ancient regimé, by whom I was surrounded, I could see without trepidation. I recall him to mind as if he were still opposite to me, seated at his little round table, of the style of Louis XV., his mantel set out with vials of all descriptions; he, bent double over the table, would from time to time raise his white head, from which would issue a low cackling sneer, creaking but not vibrating : I could not withdraw my eyes from the contemplation of this man. I knew not then that in him was the enigma of a whole age. Of the two hundred preceding years in him was the sum of the sarcastic, the denying, and the destructive ; in him was completed the age of cold and inexorable irony. He was of few words, and those were mostly monosyllables ; it would seem as if he uttered himself only to make game of language. The Revolution seemed to him but as the point of an epigram. But, notwithstanding all this, I have seen him give to the poor ; he possessed humanity ; and his deep-set eye burned with anger if a story of oppression or cruelty was related in his presence. · As to the monarchical ages, he viewed them as profoundly ridiculous, and he spoke of them as a satirist would of a bad writer. Thus the scoffing of a whole age, from Champfort to Fontenelle, was centred and condensed in this extraordinary old man. With more enthusiasm or grace, he would have been less complete : such as I saw him, he was not a man, but a negation.

He experienced in his revolutionary life one day of triumph; a great victory obtained at the point of the lance of irony and sarcasm. He was proud of it. I heard him recount this feat of arms ten times, and he had reason to boast; irony, which constituted the destructive side of the French Revolution, the most powerful side, he had employed on a certain day so apropos, he had manœuvred so skilfully, that one entire phase of the Revolution was his work. He turned the stream from the course which Robespierre had marked out. The religious idea which the last had essayed to revive, Vadier overcame by sarcasm and negation : his cutting words in a moment changed the fickle multitude, and, pronounced in the Directory, prepared the ninth of Thermidon, and killed Robespierre.

The Mystics of Deism and Naturalism, the enthusiasts of Jean Jacques, or of Swedenborg, Christians and theo-philan-thropists, did not hear of this famous triumph without horror. There were all these divisions in the wrecks of that Convention, which an allusion from history has brought out upon the canvass as Girondists and Mountains. The most divergent doctrines inflamed them all ; not systematic and meditated, but ardent and instinctive ; from thence proceeded that bitter fury which could only end in blood. Each man was a living idea, frequently vague and confused, but terrible : Anacharsis Clootz stood for the illuminism of Weisshaupt ; La Reveillère-Lèpaux, Socinianism ; Amar, *Swedenborgianism ; Vadier, irony. In an assembly so frenzied, the cold and immovable statue of irony was so extraordinary as to arrest attention.

"When the mysteries of Mother Theo are unfolded," said Vadier one day—

Amar took his hat to depart.

" Ah ! thou escapest," cried he in his cracked and Gascon voice, " the persecutor of the Mystics."

Amar said nothing, but eyed his tormentor askance, as he gently closed the door. The old man continued his recital, and recounted for the tenth time how the imbeciles ranged themselves to say mass ; how Robespierre himself—*the incorruptivle* *—(and he made this word vibrate with inimitable meridional irony) had become a bigot ; why, the *incorruptivle* put in his claims for high priest !

Continuing the same dialect and tone, he said, " By happy chance, I learned that *little mamma Theo,* (Theos, God,) summoned her little congregation in a granary ; and I braced my shoulder to the work ! and I made them frisk and leap, didn't I ? and—"

---

* Thus he pronounced the word.

"We know that story," said the good little Robert Lindet, somewhat impatiently. "You have told it us a hundred times."

"Ah! ah!" continued the Voltairian, straightening himself in spite of his gout, "when I made my report, fanaticism was struck down at a blow—it was long before it could lift up its head; and *Rovespierre* annihilated—finished—sank in the abyss! I have done it!"

And he buried himself again in his cushions with triumphant joy.

AMAR, THE SWEDENBORGIAN.

When the allies entered Paris, and the return of the Bourbons was announced as probable, a great panic seized those families who had cause for fear, or thought they had. My father and I had frequent intercourse with some of his ancient colleagues. It was at that time I became intimately acquainted with him who had been styled the ferocious Amar, and he was to me a subject of curious study.

There could be nothing more pleasant or courteous than this so-called tiger; his ancient habits, as king's treasurer and man of the world, were clearly visible in his language and manners. He spoke low; a large diamond ring which he wore, and which was sometimes, I thought, not unwittingly displayed, betrayed the financier; the finest and whitest of linen, with ruffles and bosoms embroidered and plaited in the handsomest style, with his other vestments of clear and modest shades, but not mournful, were all in keeping. At first sight, all who recollected or had studied the eighteenth century would have taken him for an economist of the sect de Quesnay. Nevertheless, his large pale face, his fair hair becoming gray, his head inclined, which seemed hesitating between reverie and calculation, his rayless blue eyes, which seemed to view nothing exterior, but gazed inwardly, impressed one with solemnity and almost with fear. Here was evinced an intellect more profound but less complete than that of Vadier. The last was possessed of an intellect keen and cutting, of which you soon took the gage ; but you knew not what force and depth were concealed beneath the calm, gentle, and meditative exterior of Amar. Some expressions of his which seemed mysterious, that were engraved on my memory in childhood, I now comprehend.

I have always remarked that the dwelling of a man has a peculiar analogy with his dispositions and tendencies. One must be a mystic or philosopher to love an extended horizon, overlooking vineyards and groves, meadows and gardens; such aspects of nature have a peculiar charm for meditative spirits, whom great cities with their eternal bustle weary and oppress.

In the third story of a house in la rue Cassette, the ancient treasurer of the king, become republican, had selected a retreat, which offered a perspective of this description. The greatest simplicity and the most perfect order prevailed within ; I recollect the windows of his study opened upon one of the most beautiful views in Paris. When a child, I was frequently sent to his house, and the sweetmeats and cakes with which he treated me could not fail to render these errands agreeable. The impression he made upon me was that of a timid recluse, who had, contrary to his tastes, left the region of abstractions, and descended into the world of realities. He manifested his emotions only by a slight and sudden blush, and a certain dilation of the pupils of the eye. This great calm, sad and gentle, could not consist with many ideas ; surely such as were concealed under such an envelope should be profound and ineffaceable. Shortly after the entrée of the allies into Paris, I went to see him, and found him more agitated than was usual with him ; he was at the same time more dressed. He was arrayed in a bright chocolate suit, with a white dimity vest, which shone in the sun. It was a suit that he wore in his youth. The window of his study was open, and a ray of light fell upon an ebony representation of Christ. Upon the bureau, opposite the two little windows, an enormous volume was opened.

As to the dweller in the cabinet, or rather cell, I met him, his head bent forward a little, his arms crossed behind, pacing the room with quick steps ; when I entered he looked at me with a peculiar smile, which seemed expressive of commiseration for my youth. Leaning upon my shoulders with his two heavy hands, his rose-tinted nails as carefully cut as those of a lady, he looked at me fixedly, as a magnetizer contemplates his subject.

" Poor little one !" cried he. " Poor soul !"

Then with a mysterious air he closed the door, and bolted it. I felt an undefined alarm in presence of this singular person ; it was not his reputation that awed me, it was he himself.

"Come along, child," said he ; "seat yourself by this bureau, and read."

I obeyed him.

The large volume of which I have spoken was before me, bound in black, ornamented with marks of all colours. This precious book, much read, and filled with notes, was no other than the "New Jerusalem" of Swedenborg, the most mystic of all mystical books, as is well known. At the moment when I began reading chapter fourth, he, continuing his walk, stopped before me, and laying his hand extended over the page, which was concealed, he exclaimed, "This is the great book, young man ; this is the teacher. The present generation comprehend it not. Happy our children if they will hearken. It is this which has directed my life ; it is the only interpreter of the Christian mysteries ; it is the grand revolutionizer."

Thus the ferocious Amar was a Swedenborgian mystic : this was the *primum mobile* and secret source of all his conduct. He willed, as Robespierre and Clootz, to regenerate humanity in spite of herself. During half an hour, concealed in the depths of a large embroidered easy-chair, which would have figured in the saloon of the treasurer of the king at Angers, he listened, smiling, and with his eyes cast upwards, to my reading of the angels of the third heaven, and their life, such as Swedenborg has revealed it upon his faith as an eyewitness.

"Ah !" cried he at length, rising with a quick and impet-

2

uous movement, not common in him, "see what men would have become if we had persevered to the end ; if we had dared ! But," added he, lowering his tone, and speaking with a cold conviction that made me tremble, "we have not done enough ; and I ask pardon of God."

He wept.

————◆————

RECOLLECTIONS OF YOUTH.

The prison in 1815.

WE have all tasted of the prison ; your experience has been mine—the universal lot. It is quite a vulgar glory: our fathers have opened the path ; may our sons lose it. I fervently hope they will witness that blessed age when the word prison will fill them with horror ; when they will shudder upon hearing of the arrest of a neighbour, and will scarcely credit the recitals of 1793, 1815, and 1848 ; when the savage scenes at the castle of Ham, Vincennes, and the Bastile, will seem as phantasmagorias of a fabulous age.

Look around ; you will find some traces of the prison in your family; you will find them even if you have led a life the most incurious and obscure ; but be not proud of these honours,——they are part of the biographical luggage of each one ; they are inscribed upon our lives as baptism and birth.

I was a child when the name of Ham echoed in my ear ; recitals of the scenes enacted there were the terror and amusement of our domestic circle. I knew her towers, her corridors, her tortuous staircases, her cells and ramparts, as if I had built them. My father had familiarized me with the dungeon in which he was confined for some long tedious months. He said : "Her Majesty the Directory had imprisoned him, and her Majesty the People did not draw him out." He dwelt upon the secret springs of the politics of the time. He described the amusements of the prisoners in the court ; their Grecian tragedies and Roman comedies enacted in the prison yard; the character of the prisoners, their hopes, their past course ; the part they had taken in the revolutionary movement, and how I came to be called Philarète, a name much too ambitious for me, but it was suggested at that time from reading Anacharsis the Younger. Oh ! how I hearkened to the stories of that terrible epoch, father of our enfeebled age, yet how different ! The convictions were then ardent, and frequently resulted in self-sacrifice ; now we have no convictions, but fruitless hypotheses. Then crimes and virtues were serious, and the seal was affixed to them by sublime or atrocious acts ; now our good and bad qualities resemble a parody; we place ourselves in a theatrical attitude. Then faith excused our errors, and enhanced our virtues ; now reigns sophistry and doubt, with individual vanity; we decorate ourselves with the tattered shreds of heroism, and strut upon the stage thinking ourselves sublime.

The stories of the chateau of Ham were engraved on my heart ; the shadow of the turrets darkened my young dreams, when a reality—a true prison—interrupted my studies, tore

me from my classics, and revealed to me the age in which I
lived.

I am sorry to be the hero of my story, not on account
of the sufferings I have endured, but as soon as you enter
this egotistic path, your personality engrosses you.   The
me becomes the tyrant, and urges you on.   How shall I
express myself, and give reality to my theme, without entering
into minute and circumstantial details, and wearying my
readers with personalities ?   In the mean time this is not my
fault ; I was unwittingly dashed into the political whirlpool,
as leaves are tossed in the tempest.   My life might have been
a wreck, but I provoked not the raging billows ; if I braved
them, it was the romance of childhood, rather than strength
and courage.

In the month of April, 1815, there were many conspiracies
in Paris.   They were ill contrived, ill woven ; concerted by
the infatuated, aided by the men who should have punished,
and excited by those who did punish them.   This was the last
refinement of politics.   My crippled father, whose leg was
wounded from the bursting of a bomb, had withdrawn from
the political arena and lived in complete solitude at the extremity of Paris.   He had purchased the old Havacourt
hotel, which had domiciled illustrious men—M. Michelet, old
Dr. Pinel, M. Mèrimèe.   There the rumour of wars, triumphs,
defeats, of monarchies reformed, overthrown, and revived,
reached us as the report of a large and distant city in flame,
and awakened as little sensibility as that would in a hermit
in his cave.   I was, I acknowledge, much more occupied with

Madame de Staël's Germany, a book that had just appeared, than with all the conspiracies of Europe. My education commenced at five years of age, before my mind opened ; and my father, a sincere and ardent convert to the theories of Jean Jacques Rousseau, deemed himself pledged, in justice to his belief, to which he had proved faithful since 1789, to follow from point to point the evangile proclaimed by the author of Émile ; he believed with him that every man's resource should be in himself ; that the most intellectual training was of no avail, and that each one, even the richest, should earn his bread by the sweat of his brow. My aspirations were different. Thus, in my fifteenth year, he proposed to crown an education too intellectual, and pursued with ardour from the earliest age, by an apprenticeship to a manual trade.

My father hastened to fulfil his purpose ; the sooner, from the view he took of the civilized world—above all, of France , sinking funds, critical positions, a threatening future, the tempest nearing, and crowns tottering as the hut of the peasant upon the Alps in the fury of the winds. I would not believe him ; him who was as cognisant in revolutionary symptoms as a pilot of Brest in shipwrecks. His was a just view of society, though I thought it exaggerated ; but I was deluded. Look at the world as it is at this day, and see if he was wrong. Our terrors—the earth quaking under our feet—prove the truth of his auguries.

Imagine the feelings of a lad just from College, who has been crowned for Grecian versions and rhetorical declamations; who has read Rousseau, Ossian, Werter, the Genius of Christianity;

who believes himself a thinker ; who has feasted to the full upon that luxuriant poison, our philosophical romances and our romantic philosophers. Workman ! what a fall ! what a title ! what a sacrifice ! A passive filial obedience bent my neck to the yoke of this terrific paternal good sense, which, in the position of our family, might have passed for extravagance, but it was only the fanaticism of reason. Never was more visionary youth rudely thrust against the spikes and spears of practical life. I deemed myself a hero in yielding without grieving and murmuring to my hard fate ; in accepting this best guarantee against the shocks of fortune, and from the scholar who wrote useless themes, becoming the compositor to print the useful ones.

There was then in Paris a printing establishment, unique in its kind. Three broken cases of types, exiled and solitary in the second story of an obscure house, situated in rue Dauphine, upon a spot that now forms a passage of that name. There were no workmen to arrange these little creative instruments, that were to give form to thought, for the master was poor, and worse than poor ; he was the butt and sport of fortune. He was feeble and miserable in soul and body. He had been a Jacobin ; one of those beings who had been a violent partisan and passive instrument, but being tasked beyond his powers, he became a revolutionary waif. How lived he ? I am ignorant. He printed not even an almanac. In the mean time he did crawl upon the face of the earth, and his idle press and dusty types uselessly cumbered the floor. I believe that the police held this house under their immediate surveillance ; but of this my father was ignorant. He saw only in the solitude of the atelier a precious opportunity of aiding an unfortunate man, and preserving my youth from the contagion of evil example. Without living in the midst of workmen, I could become one, and obtain my art without danger to my morals. My father then chose for my master poor Jacques, proprietor of a battered press. Every morning during three months, at eight o'clock, I regularly mounted to this desolate atelier in the fourth story, to remain till three.

Here I lived alone ; here I dreamed. The lessons of the master were rare, or rather, none at all ; and when my fingers became wearied from handling the types, I seated myself with a book. Whoever has not felt disgust with labour in which the mind takes no part, can never perfectly comprehend the delights of reading. You have been engaged with the grosser elements, sand, lead, wood, blind forces which have only a passive resistance, and here the thought rays before you, searching, bold, brilliant, subtile, freighted with diamonds and fruits that will live for ever. I am not astonished that great men have sprung from the ranks of mechanics : for those who have been nurtured exclusively in saloons, litera-ture is a play, an ornament ; but for those who have handled the sword, stood at the helm, or guided the plough, knowl-edge becomes a passion, a force, a beauty, a divine love. It is from our shops, and ateliers, and notaries' offices, where are piled deeds which taxed not the mind, that issue most of our powerful spirits ; Molière from the upholsterer's shop; Burns from the plough ; Shakspeare was the son of a draper and

glover ; Rousseau worked with his father, who was a wheel-
wright.   Those   ardent   spirits, long   struggling   with   the
grosser elements, happy and enthusiastic, took refuge in the
free domain of thought.   Even an inferior mind gains strength
from an apprenticeship in the mechanic arts ; and if the great
reform which engages the thoughts of so many should ever be
effected, and should create all men citizens, I doubt not but
good sense will prevail over habit, and the most important
improvement in each one's education will consist in the development of the intellectual and physical powers in union,
and a practical application of those powers upon the elements
of nature.   I should wish all agriculturists to read, and all
rich men to practise some mechanic art ; at the present day
the ignorance of one class, and corruption of another, conceals
God and the sanctity of the human mission.   I deem the
serious study of physical nature and the knowledge of a trade
equally important for the powerful and rich, as the attainment of the French language and the study of the Bible for
our peasants, artisans, and labourers.

    Not one of these ideas entered my head at the time I have
been speaking of.   I was just from College ; I had my tragedy to compose, my reveries to indulge in, and Gessner to
read.   I carefully accomplished my task, but with what
pleasure I returned to the mawkish pastorals of Solomon
Gessner, whose vapid moralizing then appeared to me the
height of good taste and elegance !   Oh! shepherdesses of
these idyls ; Oh ! Chloe, Daphne, Leucothe! how beautifully
ye beamed upon me in my dark and sad abode, draperied

by spiders ; the little windows and small panes of which admitted only the discordant notes of the hand-organ, the distant rumbling of carriages ; within the house, from a neighbouring room, there reached my ear the agonizing screams of a poor epileptic and the angry murmurings and invectives from a party of gamblers. My curiosity was much excited by these gamblers ; every day, in the afternoon, I saw some old women, with green reticules, enter a room, from which they would issue forth at ten the next morning : thus spending the night in their orgies. On a certain day I heard a pistol shot from that room. I still see the chamber with the green carpet, across which my eyes would feign penetrate behind the red curtain which concealed the actors in the interior of the den.

Dependent upon my own resources for entertainment, I invented a means by which I could reconcile my elegiac and literary tastes with the duties which were imposed upon me; it was to print some fragments from my favourite authors, sometimes translated by myself, when they were foreign. It was in this way that I commenced the study of German, first translating, and then becoming the compositor and printer of the Hermann and Dorothéa of Gœthe. One Saturday evening, after having commenced in this manner the translation, in five hexameters, upon rhyme plates, of the Daphnis of Gessner, I left upon the press the book which had delighted me so much, which yet I could not be induced to read now, notwithstanding the associated charms. The next morning my father was to drive me into the country, five leagues

2*

from Paris. The advent of Spring, with its balmy air and
sunny smile, would not find us reluctant worshippers ; but I
could not depart without Gessner, and at seven in the morning
I was at the printing office.   Another motive united itself to
my love of Gessner in leading me to the printer's ; his wife
was poor and ill ; her son was subject to the most dreadful
of natural maladies, epilepsy : added to which, her husband
was a prey to the most deplorable of social infirmities, gloom,
envy, and fanaticism.   The interior of this house was
wretched ; it required all the *insouciance*, and dreaminess,
and illusions of fifteen, to bring my idyls there ; to mingle
with the distress, sickness, and the wretched results of
Jacobinism and revolutions the mythology of the boudoir.
I was charged with some money for the poor sick woman
from my mother.   My mother did not share in the enthusiastic opinions of my father ; a zealous Protestant, she did
works of mercy and distributed alms with that discreet zeal
and self-forgetfulness which alleviated her own manifold trials.
But this day, her alms, joined to my eclogues, opened for me
the gates of the Conciergerie.   All this trifling detail was
necessary to explain by what chain of little circumstances,
(notwithstanding my childish insignificance, and however
unworthy that honour,) I was in the sequel enclosed within
the walls of a dungeon.

On reaching the printer's that memorable morning, I saw
two men stationed in the dark passage at the foot of the
narrow tortuous staircase leading to Jacques' apartment.   I
little heeded these sentinels in threadbare coats, though they

examined me inquisitively ; but depositing my offering upon a table in a little ante-chamber, I went up to the atelier. Returning, book in hand, I perceived through the open door of a room a man with a scarf, leaning upon the mantel with a weary, indolent air. I pursued my course, and entered the wretched little chamber of Jacques to inquire for his poor wife. I was ignorant of life ; this scarf should have informed me that I had an affair. Scarcely had I entered the chamber when two men seized me ; they proceeded to search me : I was dumb with amazement. The steady and piercing eye of the adjutant of the police was fastened upon me ; my outline of a projected tragedy enclosed in a portfolio, upon which was staked my hope of immortality, was carefully secured and labelled. Next my name, age, and rank, were demanded ; notes were taken ; then, without deigning to say what they wished to do with me, or why I was arrested, these honourable gentlemen ordered me to follow them. They were dressed in black cravats, and no shirt collars ; each carried a club ; and their office was to lead their unresisting victim to the police office.

The gentlemen who escorted me were as polished as the alguazils in comedy. To the amenity of the cat and tiger, which consists in a rough play with their victims, and distinguishes those who live by human misery as well as the beast of prey, they joined, I thought, some commiseration for my youth and the simple innocence of my questions. While we were crossing the Pont-Neuf, they endeavoured to comfort and console me. The women, who by intuition discover all our pains, looked compassionately upon me. In answer to my inquiries, my guard replied that this summons was all a matter of form, and that I should soon return to my family; *that* chance which had led me to a printer accused of political dereliction, was not sufficient for detention : in fine, they made me believe I should see my poor mother again in the evening. Thus reässured, I entered fearlessly the whimsical and absurd structure called the *Police*, whose walls conceal so many plagues and moral sores. The great and terrible magistracy of Paris, the moral edileship, has omitted nothing that can make her a curse. Instead of consecrating a palace worthy of her name, she is built over a sewer. There my bailiffs quitted me, and I was roughly pushed into an oblong hall, of which the odour was suffocating.

My education had been delicate and tender to excess ; the utopian enthusiasm of my father and the adorable instructions of my mother in the tranquil solitudes of home had shielded my youth from any exposure to contemporary vices. I knew nothing of Paris. I was habituated to a simple life, innocent, beautiful, even elegant ; and here, as I looked around, I saw men half naked, women clothed in rags, their lewd eyes and blowzed faces wearing marks of the bottle and brothel ; people whom, if you met in the streets of Paris, you would feel contaminated. Here and there were some peasants in frocks, who with their arms crossed lay stretched upon the floor ; other groups smoking and playing piquet with greasy cards, seated upon the foul floor ; the stench from so many filthy people congregated around was intolerable—was horrible. Here were swarms of wretches by night and day ; no egress ; here they must eat, drink, and sleep : thus a field bedstead was supplied, which swarmed with the miserable wretches ; the poor and unhappy, the drunken, the debauched, were all piled upon each other; and this hall was dedicated to St. John ! It was here that blind policy, as cruel under the republic as when swayed by monarchy, Briareus armed, seized all in her path ; and to this infernal place my youth was hurried. I seated myself in a corner near the embrasure of a window, and wept. The slang of the thieves prevented me from comprehending any thing that was said around me ; the obscene laugh, lewd gestures, and ferocious effeminacy, special characteristic of vice in great cities, shocked my eyes, filled as they were with tears. These wretches, at the same time haggard and gay, with leer of the eye and a saucy laugh which made their odious wrinkles more visible, came close up, insulting me for my delicate and tender aspect, my tears, and scared look, as they savagely called the confusion and amazement which seized me at this unexpected scene.

A trembling old man accosted me ; he spoke with difficulty ; his lips were always open from decrepitude ; his head was totally bald, and he seemed to shake with the struggling words in their endeavour to escape. He was an ancient advocate, arrested the night before in consequence of an accusation of conspiracy ; in his debility there was to be perceived a remnant of good manners ; but his rayless soul, his voice, which was an inward muttering without the breath

of life, prevented me from comprehending his long discourse
I could only divine that our arrest was caused from the same
suspicion ; he upon the borders of the tomb, I at the threshold of life ; and we had both met in this abode of infamy ;
in the limbo of the dungeon.

Among the wretches huddled in this hall, whose sixty
visages are still before me, there was one I marked particularly as being the most peculiar and interesting of all ; he
was a fanatic. The sceptical age had not destroyed the
element of love and enthusiasm which survives for ever in
the human heart. This being was at the same time a
Catholic, a revolutionist, and a magnetizer. Drifted upon
the rue de Jerusalem, as a detached wreck from a romance
of Walter Scott, he was seized, and here he held forth,
casting the shadows of his poetic and wild dreams along
these sweepings of society—the *picked people*, as they were
called in the slang of St. John's. His face was long and
wan, and his eye kindled by enthusiasm ; his long black hair
waved in natural curls ; he wore no cravat, and his speech
was rapid, strange, and incoherent. He preached to those
around him, who blasphemed in listening, I know not what
Christian heresy of the recreation of society. He predicted
that this new order of society was to arise from the triple
power of magnetism, Christ, and Robespierre. He left a
peculiar and deep impression upon the mind of the child as
of a person intrusted with a mission to this assembly. There
seemed united a flaccidity and softness of the muscular
parts in the frame of this monomaniac, which usually

attaches to irregular habits. He was seized at the corner of a street, preaching to the bystanders. I do not know what became of him.

Vermin infested the crowded bed, and I preferred passing my night in a chair within the embrasure of the window. The next morning the jailer distributed the rations to the prisoners ; to each one was given a slice of black bread. I asked permission to write to my mother—the most tender of mothers, who was suffering from illness, and had received no tidings from me. I was refused.

Cut off from the outward world, my sad life, my anxiety, the wretched scenes around me, and distress for my mother, brought on a fever in three days. At length the jailer obtained permission for me to write. I wrote two letters— one to my mother, and one to the prefect of the police ; but I was obliged to despatch them unsealed, according to the rule in these places. In the evening an answer from my mother reached me, and with it a ring from her, which I have always kept. The next morning at twelve my name was called at the grate, which was a summons to the interrogation.

After three days and three nights passed without sleep, and in that stupor of grief which is easy to imagine, my nervous system was violently excited. We failed in water in this hall of *picked* people. My linen was soiled, my outer garments shabby and unfit to appear in, and my fever raged. I was placed between two gendarmes. Through many dark corridors, up stairs and down stairs, through winding passages, turn within turn in our tortuous course, we at length reached the notary's office in a lower room. I heard a cry; my mother had risen from the bed of illness, and come to embrace me a moment. The indulgence of the police permitted her to see me, and no more ; she embraced me without speaking ; she looked at me, and her wistful glance said, how much you are changed. No more was permitted ; she was ordered to withdraw, and led away. The paleness of my mother and her tears gave me a shock which I cannot express. For a long time she had been given over by the physicians. Her heart was diseased; but Corvisart prolonged her life. He told her that violent emotions would destroy her, and it seemed to be by an artificial process that this delicate plant was preserved. A native of Sedan, descended from an old Friesland and Dutch family, whose chiefs, as their names indicate, (Halma, Alma, with the oriental aspiration,) belonged to the Arabian wreck, conquered by Charles Martel, she had inherited from her patriarchal race a love for old institutions and ancient usages. Beautiful as an angel, she was married at eighteen to an ardent royalist; they spent the honeymoon of their wedded life in the dungeons of Sedan, and then the young wife saw her husband perish upon the scaffold. Her second husband, my father, was an ardent republican. Adrift in stormy seas, they were both glad to anchor their little barque in some peaceful haven.

Before a desk, filled with parchments carefully piled and numbered, was seated in his arm-chair a man whose name I knew not, but who represented a class, that of tools of the government. His face was short and square, swarthy and wrinkled, at the same time fat and bony; his low forehead was shortened still more by the peruke which he wore; his eyebrows were bushy, his skin wrinkled at the corners of his eyes, his shoulders like a hangman, with mien of an inquisitor; he was my jury and judge. I remained standing before this doughty man, who abruptly began his interrogations and vituperations. "Monsieur, you belong to a species that must be cut off; a race of vipers! There will be no peace in France till they are crushed."

In politics, all races who do not think with us are vipers. In 1793, the defenders of Louis XVI.; in 1799, the friends of Carnot; in 1805, the partisans of the Bourbons; in 1815, the believers in liberty were the races of vipers. I was surprised at this language, and my reasoning powers were precociously awakened.

"But, Monsieur," replied I with puerile haughtiness, "I thought you were going to question me upon facts, and I hear only abuse." This doughty man, whom my shabby and torn dress, together with my puny appearance, encouraged in his insults, now bounded from his leathern chair, as a tiger caught in a snare, and rising in all his littleness, and thumping the desk with his doubled fist, he cried,

"Eh! will *you* teach *me* what I am to do? You lecture *me*, Monsieur." I have not forgotten one of his words.

"I will just remind you, Monsieur," replied I, coolly, "that your business is not with a criminal, neither with a person accused of guilt, but with an innocent young man, who

knows not why he is here, by what right imprisoned, or under
what pretext detained."

"It is," returned the interrogator, reseating himself, "because you make such fine speeches. You belong, as may be
easily seen, to the young liberals. Register, record all that
Monsieur says."

Then chafing himself in his harness, as the arrogance of
my replies augmented his anger, and not being able to obtain
from me any clue to the conspiracies of which he sought the
track, for I was a stranger to all political intrigues, and
execrated the name of politics, (a feeling which I have preserved intact to the present day,) this hunter of men,
wrathful at not being able to entrap me, took a more direct
path ; he opened my confiscated portfolio and commented ·
upon my rough sketch of William Tell. Some verses of my
fragments were dedicated to liberty ; and the first couplet of
a miserable liberal ode, traced with a pencil, was alleged
against me, and I was questioned upon my secret intentions,
my ideas, and theories ; and since facts failed him, he took
care to inveigle me in my replies. He asked me if I loved
the reigning dynasty ; I was silent a moment, and I then
said to him with firmness a little emphatic, which I explain
now from my early and precocious reading, with its romantic
taint : "I know not, Monsieur, as I love any government ;
I have lately left college, and I cannot reply to these
questions of theory and personal affection. This sort of interrogation, according to my idea, surpasses the functions in
which you acquit yourself so well. As to the verses written

in my portfolio, they are some fragments from a tragedy which I shall read to the committee of the Odeon ; they have no connection with the police, and you would do justice if you would restore me to my family, from whence I was arrested under so puerile a pretext."

Fury seized him.

"Impertinent reasoner ! know you that I can at this moment send you to the dungeon ?" He ordered me to sign a paper in which was recorded, not all that I had said, but the material part of my replies ; and upon a signal from Monsieur, the gendarme led me away to another chamber, in which was an officer of about forty years, who wore the cross of the Legion of Honour. He was accused of conspiracy, and looked upon me with compassion and tenderness, at the same time offering me his hand.

"Ah !" said he, "do they accuse you of conspiracy ? Of what age are you, young man ?"

"Fourteen !"

"This is strange." The Colonel threw himself upon his bed, and remained long silent.

In the evening two gendarmes came for me in a hack ; they told me to get in, then one placed himself each side of me, and I was driven to the Palace of Justice, whose court at that time led to the entrance of the famous *Conciergerie!* Near the large steps which lead to the palace, you discover in a corner to the right a double grating sunk under ground, which conceals the deep dungeons of the Conciergerie ; the weight of the superincumbent buildings seemed to press upon them

as society crushes the victims, innocent or guilty, who are
buried therein. Is this a prison, a sewer, a cellar ? You cannot say ; this door of the prison, so low, so narrow, so black,
was overshadowed by the projections of the surrounding edi-
fices. At the grate was stationed the guard of the hell within ;
to the right hung the calendar, or jailer's book ; before you
burns, with a feeble gleam, the sombre lamp, which, like a
stream of blood, casts its lurid glare along the funereal avenue.

I entered, preceded by a gendarme, followed by a gendarme. My first impression was of death and the tomb.
Afterwards, (I confess to the sin of the tragedy hero, but I
was educated in France, and among *us* all is theatrical,) this
flagrant iniquity inspired me with courage, and, in view of
those craven souls who stood in fear of my childhood, I felt
myself elevated to the precocious dignity of a martyr. The
consciousness of the pure and elevated feelings and pursuits
which engrossed me when surprised by the adjutant of the
police, conviction of my own innocence, the disgust with
which such barbarity inspired me—perhaps the whimsical
pleasure of feeling that I in my early years should struggle
against ills the most poignant and bitter that maturity could
grapple with—strangely exalted me. I felt that I should be
equal to any suffering or affliction which could hereafter
befall me, and that I could withstand it all. I threw the
glove of defiance at all evils, seen or unseen, which should
beset my path, and it has aided me, for I have suffered much
in life, (I say it in passing,) but, above all, through my mind
and affections.

My name was inscribed in the jailer's book ; that fact is attended with ignoble fear ; it proclaims you subdued by physical force ; a chain is rivetted around you : handcuffed and fettered, you are brought to prison as a thief.   You become the butt of the keeper, you descend from the condition of the man to that of the idol and the brute ; you are classed, cribbed, labelled ; you are as the trunk of a once noble tree, hewn down, separated from its brethren of the forest, and ignobly piled in the outbuilding of its owner.

The lantern in the doorway threw a feeble and doubtful light upon the objects around.   I saw the tattered shreds of a thief, who, seated upon the bench with me, waited to have his name registered ; then a large man in a brown jacket seized my hand.   We ascended staircases, passed along corridors,——the damp wind whistled in these dark passages ; my eyes, unaccustomed to this new world, only saw isolated, flickering red spots, waving from distance to distance : these were the lamps attached to the walls.

" We have our orders, young man," said the jailer ; " you are for the secret cell.   I am sorry."

" What is the secret cell ?"

" It is a place you cannot quit, and you can see no one."

We went down many steps which led to a long corridor, ventilated by spiracles ; many iron bars were opened to give us passage, and fell back, reverberating ; the third door of the corridor opened into my dungeon, which was secured by a massive iron door, guarded with all the bolts which the special luxury of those places demand.

"This is your cell," said the jailer, after raising two iron bars, and turning three times the enormous key whose dissonant creaking long grated in my ear.

My cell was eight feet long, five broad, and twelve in height, very dark ; one side of the wall the briny water was dripping down ; another side there was a wooden partition ; the floor was beat hard as a cellar ; above the door, fifteen feet from the floor, was an iron lattice, three feet broad and one high, which admitted an obscure light ; but this mockery of a window was shaded by a blind on the outside. These were ingenious precautions ! In a corner to the right, opposite the door, were scattered some tresses of old matted straw ; below the window stood a bucket ; near the door, to the left, another bucket, filled with water, and a wooden porringer. I was appalled—I felt a cold shudder. This was the prison of the condemned, the dungeon in all its horror that was allotted to me at my age, when I was not even attainted, or suspected of crime.

Although the authors of this melo-drama had abused their power, I felt tempted to believe in the commiseration of the jailers ; they see so few cases deserving of pity! and when they chance to meet with one, habituated as they are to the sight of suffering, and wearied with apathy, they enjoy the relaxation of a little compassion,—of a passing charity. Claude pitied me, and served me well. His wooden figure seemed to dilate and take a softer mould in observing me, and he lingered when I spoke to him ; and it was good for me could I detain him even five minutes. This man in brown jacket and leathern girdle, loaded with keys, was more merciful than the interrogator, a man of the world, who dined out, wore black silk breeches, and talked with the ladies. Now Monsieur's wounded self-love was revenged ; glutted to the full.

I remained in the dungeon ; some prison-bread was brought me, hard and black ; added to which, it was of an odour so absolutely revolting, that even my hunger could not induce me to touch it.

"Do you wish the pistole ?" said Claude. When I had ceased weeping, I asked his meaning. For one hundred francs per month I might obtain a bed, white bread, some nutritious food, a table and a chair. But I thought only of my home, and I asked Claude if I could not communicate with my family.

"I will send some one," said he, "to bring you news of your mother ; but it is forbidden you to write or receive letters." I gave Claude to understand that my father would not fail to pay the pistole, and to recompense any services rendered to me ; and I asked him to say to my family that my health was good and I was tranquil. When, in the evening, going his nightly rounds, barring the doors and attending to the ordinary cares of a prison, he reached my cell, he told me that he had seen my mother, that she remained a long time in the parlour talking to him, and had given him fruit to bring to me. Her maternal grief had touched the heart of Claude. He brought me the *pistole*, consisting of a tottering table of light wood, a rush-bottomed chair, damp sheets, and a paltry little gray couch, on the back of which was traced with a pencil these words : *M. de Labédoyère has slept here the*—the rest was effaced.   He was the unhappy Colonel de Labédoyère, who three days before had quitted this bed to march to that of death.

In a few days my dungeon was enlivened a little by some books which were sent to me.   I had written to my father, but without sealing my letter, and asked him to send me some old books : Mabillon and Ariosto, Sauval and Jean Jacques, Saint-Foix and Werther.   I now commenced my prison studies by an examination of ancient writers.   From mere listlessness, and having nothing better to do, I made extracts from those who had collected the historical wrecks of our cities.   Not one among them has accomplished his task poetically, and it is pitiful to see with what doleful and merciless exactitude they registered and with what elaborate subtility they reasoned upon the ancient monuments, without seizing the real life of the extinguished people.   I was interested, however, in deciphering from their cold pages something upon the ancient design of my Conciergerie.

The Conciergerie, the Palace, the City, was the ancient Lutèce ; there were the loves of Julian.   This little island, first inhabited by boatmen, is the centre of modern Paris. My thought reverted to the germ of this great city.   I saw, in my reverie, the guard-house of the Roman Citadel ; I saw the pit where criminals of the municipal city were immured, without form of trial, by the Roman centurions.   Afterwards, this prison was extended to a subterranean hall, under the tower of the military chiefs.   By degrees, as turrets and halls were added, and the building acquired splendour, the subterranean hall was enlarged, dungeons multiplied. The palace under Robert II. was an edifice of *signal* beauty, (said Heligond,) that is to say, it was a square tower, flanked with bastions. Fortress, royal residence, and prison ; this was the feudal *community*, consisting in physical force, priestly hierarchy, and military despotism. The chiefs of the primitive race, foolishly called kings by our own historians, chiefs of savage tribes and armies, defiled before me ; I beheld their whimsical court, composed of Gallic bishops and Leudes ;* of warriors leagued with them ; captives taken in war swelled the triumph ; then, descending the course of ages, I come to Saint Louis, who built the palace anew, with a long row of Gothic colonnades, not forgetting the kitchens ; and Philip the Fair, who followed the example of his predecessor, and aggrandized still more this royal domain. These were the lessons I conned ; facts which I gathered, and which loomed up through the hazy atmosphere of the Abbé Lebœuf, M. Sauval, and other archæologists.

Thus the first germ of Paris, the queen city, the cradle of society, the nucleus which enclosed the future of a whole population, and the pivot of a great city, was a prison. From the little island of Lutèce, still the heart of Paris, the city enlarged, houses and palaces multiplied, and entire vil-

---

* A name given in ancient days to great vassals who voluntarily followed their chief to war.

3

lages were absorbed. But what a lesson ! As soon as the
city took form the dungeon was excavated ; Lutèce had no
ramparts, but she had her prison ; perhaps the cell allotted
to me was the first dungeon. In this subterranean abode,
which cradled the queen city, how much anguish has been
concealed. This abode, consecrated to tears and misery,
has since been called Conciergerie.

If I have for a long time felt the most entire indifference
for the movements of modern society ;—if I have opposed
the hopes of progress manifested by my best friends, it is not
from heartless scepticism, but a firm negation ;—if I have
proclaimed from the moment of taking the pen, the imminent
decline of Christian Europe, especially France, which has
lost the sense of justice and the idea of God,—it may be
easily explained by referring to my imprisonment, which was
the commencement of my moral life. I meditated long and
deeply under those humid walls. But my historical studies
were not of long duration ; they soon gave place to reveries
more romantic ; often to thoughts more sad ; and they both
engrossed my long nights and mournful days, in which there
was no outward change from day to day, from week to week.
Reverie is the only luxury in a prison. I read Ariosto,
stretched upon my sorry couch, my elbows leaning upon the
tottering table which held my books. I scribbled some
foolish verses, and wrote long sentimental and Ossianic pages,
the custom at that time, as true in sentiment as false in
style. It is thus the young write. I read Pamela, a failure
from a man of genius ; the moral is false from prudery. Then

through the pages of the sweet Tasso an angel spirit had devised a means of communicating with the youth of fourteen, by underlying many of the words, so as to form sentences, which the youth only could interpret.

My eyes accustomed themselves in three days to the very feeble and sparing light that the spiracle dispensed to me. But the emotions of the young man were often too powerful to be dissipated by books of history or romance. The first evening of my imprisonment, when all the bars fell, prolonging their echo through the long vaults, I shuddered ; my isolation looked me in the face ; I was as one dead, who awakens suddenly to find his tomb closed upon him. The next morning a porringer of milk was brought to me ; I could not restrain my tears ; I contrasted this solitary repast with the breakfast at home ; and to the little lunch that I would carry into the large garden, and, perched upon a tree, eat the bread whilst reading Werter. Sometimes I heard a heavy carriage stop, the hinges would creak, the gates roll back, the bars of the dungeon fall ; there was tumult in the prison, then all still as death ;—a new prisoner had been brought.

My cell was below the level of the court or prison-yard; over this yard were the windows, or rather perforations intended to admit a glimmer of light, and slightly ventilate the *Souricière*, a filthy abomination, containing a corrupt mass of human flesh. The Souricière was divided into parts for the two sexes, and it was, I believe, a provisionary prison where criminals were heaped pell-mell, awaiting a more exact division. The Souricière for females was near enough to my cage for sounds to reach me from thence, and often words. There were love songs sung in any thing but harmonious strains ; sometimes horrible blasphemies uttered in sweet and youthful tones ; obscene narrations from young girls ; stories of robbery and murder with all a culprit's slang ; added to these were ballads, boat songs, and bacchanalian tunes, mixed with imprecations, curses of rage, and shouts of laughter.. What was most sad in the scene was the reckless gaiety ; never were Bohemians more merry ; all sadness, all remorse, all ideas of decency and virtue were banished from these women who were the dregs of society and steeped in iniquity. Pardon me these details, which seem frivolous only to frivolous people. This transformation of the human soul impressed me strongly. I shall never forget it, and a large portion of my ideas and studies have resulted from my prison life. I have from that time denied that the system of society was right, that man is an angel, and can dispense with God, or substitute another. I was initiated in no vice; crime was revealed to me only from history, and seen under the shadow of a deep and vague perspective. My innocent childhood was a species of Idyl; I was absorbed in visions and reveries, only interrupted by occasional paternal declamations. My childhood, cradled in poetic visions, luxuriating in Gessner, Ossian, and Paul and Virginia, had not prepared me for these frightful revelations. They terrified me as a lurid flame from the tombs. When I heard one of the women sing the popular melody of the Italian Catruffo, *Charming Picture*, &c., the contrast was too strong and the dissonance too painful; I could not hear her sing that air.

One day I heard more stir and bustle than usual in prison; the bell tolled longer; I heard steps; a clashing of bayonets; the prison door next to mine was opened and shut several times; then there were sobs and groans in that cell. When Claude came into my dungeon he wore his uniform, and was serious. The sobs and cries from the next cell increased in intensity; but the women of the Souricière sang without intermission. I learned from the jailer that a prisoner condemned to death occupied the cell contiguous to mine; that the day for execution had arrived, and the hour had struck ; that the sad confessions of the unhappy wretch occasioned the sobs and groans ; the priest was there, and the condemned, on his knees, phrenzied through intoxication and despair, had received absolution, and there was only ten minutes between life and death. Now all the bells began anew their funereal knell; the rumbling of wheels shook the earth and the prison; the murmur of distant voices echoed from the distant train;—a few moments, and the quiet of the dungeon succeeded to this tumult.

A sensitive organization of fourteen could not resist the evil effects of a dungeon life; the privation of air and exercise, sorrow at not seeing those whom I loved, the sad scenes around me which left an ineffaceable impression, together with the humid atmosphere, did its work, and I became ill. A month had thus passed when the physician petitioned that I should walk in the prison-yard.

I was led by Claude into an oblong court, excavated ten or twelve feet below the surrounding streets, overshadowed by lofty structures, and secured by high stone walls barbed with iron spikes. Many prisoners with naked and dirty feet were pacing the prison-yard ; all stared at me; some with hairy, brawny arms gathered round me, rudely and roughly inquiring who I was; many in shirts, with no other clothing than coarse gray cloth pantaloons, were stretched upon the sable soil, shouting and playing cards: some of the prisoners were at work upon little fancy articles of straw, of which the delicacy was extreme. I encountered vice, not such as I had seen it in the hall of St. John; less petulant, more resolute, hardened, vindictive, and hideous. In the police hall you saw a torn cravat; vice wore her tattered shreds; used a language of some pretension ; was semi-social, and had some of the habits of civilization; but here was no disguise; vice, if I may so say, displayed herself in her perfection, studied her attitudes, ornamented herself with her shreds, and redoubled her energy. Her only dialect was slang; malignant irony without mercy. A blasting scorn was depicted upon their visages; the eyes of the gamblers seemed to shoot forth hellish flame. In the centre of Paris; in the midst of a consolidated and polished society, but concealed by high walls, is this barbarous community, who have borrowed from civilization her skill and craft, and employed them against civilization. I was more appalled at these wretches' faces, gestures, and jargon than I should have been at the scaffold.

Twice I walked in this prison-yard; the third walk was in

another yard much smaller, of oblong form, and it resembled the bottom of a well with a high wall around.   In the cells which lead out from a low narrow passage to this little court were many accused of political crimes ; amongst others a lieutenant of the cavalry, with cheeks of a reddish brown, gray moustaches; he was always in good humour, reckless, giddy ; his health was proof against every exposure ; he amused himself with innocent railleries against his persecutors, and behind his iron grating made himself merry by singing and telling amusing stories.   I breathed the air three times in eight days; then it was perceived my health was sufficiently restored, and I returned to the dungeon and darkness.

The unfortunate persons engaged in the conspiracy to which it was pretended I was knowing, were condemned to exile or the scaffold.*

One morning, my juvenile stoicism subdued, I was lying weeping upon my couch, listening to the neighbouring bells of Notre Dame, and contemplating sadly an oblique ray of sunshine which found its way through the spiracle to my

---

* It may be asked, Why a child so inoffensive as I was should have been so oppressed ?   At a later day I discovered the cause.   There was promulgated a proclamation pretending to be from Marie-Louise, and the police-agent plied all his forces to discover the culprit author ; and after three days' useless search he became angry.   At length I was discovered, and taken for a true printer's boy, as the adjutant of the police had so designated me.   My dress was plain, and ten days' imprisonment had not improved its appearance.   When he discovered my parentage, he thought he had the clue by which he might trace the writer, and from my simplicity he hoped to obtain the secret.

dungeon,—the sound of steps more heavy and rapid than usual struck my ear. Every thing is exact in a prison; a jailer regularly keeps the same pace, like the pendulum of a clock, never hurrying his steps. Claude turned quickly the large key of my door, and said,

" You have only to come out, there is a carriage waiting."

I knew not, in truth, what to do with my liberty, so much did this news stun me; and I cannot render a just account of my sensations and ideas during an entire day. Claude did up my little packet; and I was driven home. I found my mother in her bed, extremely ill; but I remember, as if it were but yesterday, her tears and kisses ; also the life-inspiring freshness of the lovely May, and the fragrance and sweet odours of the garden where I embraced my father. I never shall forget the deep emotion of the old man; the tears which fell upon me as they coursed down his furrowed cheeks, and the strange intoxication which, after a month's darkness and isolation, made me tremble violently, and seemed ready to destroy life from the excess of new life and happiness. I recall, also, the words of. my father, as proudly leaning upon the crutch which supported his shortened and wounded leg, stationed in the centre of his green lawn, his glowing face uplifted, as if addressing a popular assembly, or occupying his old chair of rhetoric :

" My son," said he, emphatically, " the land of France is too hot for you. You can do nothing here; day after to-morrow you must depart for England.   France is decaying, sinking; all Europe will follow. Jean Jacques, our apostle and master, predicted it. You have served your apprentice-ship as Æmilius; and it only remains for you, like him, to wind up the whole by a tour."

According to his directions I departed from home; my month's imprisonment decided my destiny. The diverse details of circumstances which procured my enlargement can have no interest excepting for myself. Without entering into egotistic details, which I abhor, I will just say that M. de Châteaubriand, upon the intercession of an angel, demanded my liberation. The voice of a man of genius and the tears of a young girl, united, wrought my emancipation.

. . . .

In 1832 I felt impelled to visit, or I may say I was drawn towards the dungeon in which I had passed two months; it was a summons from my soul——a call of the spirit to return to the past, to the remembrance of friends and companions in 1815, of whom I alone survived. God knows, in fifteen years, how the graves surge around man! The grate where my mother wept spoke to me of her. The darkness, con-fidant of my fears, deep emotions, and affections, would re-open the spring that the cold had frozen.

And where were you, Conciergerie, black and lugubrious, impassable witness of the Revolution ; horrible staircases, dark passages oozing with the dampness of the sepulchre ? Time, which changes men, moves stones : the prison of 1815 had vanished. I saw the new Conciergerie of 1831, but I no more found *my jail* in this philanthropic prison: this was a grief to me.

3*

Now you do not enter the Conciergerie through the court of the Palace of Justice. There is no longer the low door half buried in the earth, nor sepulchral lamp; but the ingress and egress is near the Quai de l'Horloge, and is like that of a lordly manor. On your path to the prison you pass through the kitchens of St. Louis, and through long Gothic and majestic halls, of which the height is remarkably diminished by the filling up of the soil. The whole character of the place has changed; the staircases are commodious. The air circulates; the pistole is a sinking fund; you would take the keepers for the attendants and nurses of an hospital. I have seen five or six women walking very quietly in the court-yard. The bread distributed to the prisoners is good enough for soldiers ; and I believe there are few vestiges of the ancient cruelty of prisons. This one now resembles a well-kept hospital. The social changes in France put all upon a level: commoners and the nobility, the shop and the saloon. All civilization proceeds upon the idea of the people's rights; and there is no line of separation between crime and innocence or infirmity; the house of chastisement is like the retreat for the sick and infirm; the health of the respected criminals, carefully guarded, attests the *progress* of *society*. Our civilization perfects itself at the risk of its own destruction. I acknowledge the amelioration, but I had wished to spend some hours alone in my cell of 1815.

The moral aspect of the jail has not changed. The Souricière sing always; the prison-yard is the same. The great problem of reforming vice fomented in the capitals is not resolved. The philanthropists have cleansed the outside without affecting the interior life.

When I quitted prison I already felt previsions of the decay of France. Even as a boy I had a vague feeling of the chaotic state of society ; from utopian she became flagitious, from false, impious ; I felt that her moral sense was lost, and the love of God extinguished.

A week later and I was in London, in the land of the faithful ; amongst a people submitting to law even to the point of superstition—loyal, religious, but with less brilliancy, less genius than my countrymen.

SOME RECOLLECTIONS OF M. DE CHATEAUBRIAND.

In 1817 chance carried me to a spot where Chateaubriand had resided in 1798. Living in poverty and obscurity, sad even to despair, by sickness brought to the gates of death, without friends or hope, the great exile left only feeble traces of himself in some minds. I have questioned the few who could give me information, and I now relate the result.

I perceived Chateaubriand to be more real, that is, more truly great than he is commonly believed ; neither apostate, apostle, sceptic, or fanatic ; not a worldly and ambitious man, nor an ascetic ; nothing of all that ;—but a gentleman educated in the doctrines of Jean Jacques, a passionate disciple of Æmilius ; an ardent admirer of savage life, and very inimical to the state of society of the eighteenth century ; but he had become a sincere and ardent Christian.

This point of departure of M. de Chateaubriand was very common ; like Madame de Staël, Napoleon, Coleridge, and Goëthe, he became sick of negation, which is so sterile. Before he detached himself, he had been, not sceptical, but a *denier*, with all the vehemence of Raynal ; and he took the resolution to go to America, to confirm by the sweat of his brow his faith in the excellence of the savage life and the greatness of primitive man : he returned to England still in the same faith.

I heard him spoken of when I was in London by the architect, M. Porden, who in his person was a complete epitome of the past : a preserved mummy ; his black silk breeches fell in longitudinal plaits over his lank knees, which were perfectly sharp ; indeed, he was made up of angles, body and spirit.

As an architect he was a born Gothic ; he made his fortune by minarets. In his anathema against colonnades he scrupled not to call Homer—*dotard*, and M. de Chateaubriand—*charlatan*.

One day that Brown, Porden, and myself dined together at the table of the old bookseller Baylis, they questioned me with regard to my transient abode in the Conciergerie, passages in my life of which the English can hardly be made to understand the why and wherefore.

" And who took you out of prison ?" said Porden.

" M. de Chateaubriand," I replied.

" Ah ! don't speak to me of him," said the old architect. " I have known him as republican, sentimentalist, Wertherian, declaimer, deist, and jacobin. There is a beautiful upholder of monarchy ! and a faithful high-priest for Catholicism !"

After this ebullition, the angry man appeased, briskly pushed the decanter around, swallowed his glass of claret, smacked his lips, buried his hands in his breeches pockets of rusty old black silk, and threw himself back in his chair, winking his eyes, as if he had achieved a great triumph. Negation was the joy of his heart. In point of poetry, he liked Crabbe ; in architecture the ogive : all which was not pointed, sharp, or at least angular, ill suited him.

"No, speak not of him," continued he, whilst old Baylis looked at him smiling ; "I know why General Bonaparte saw him with an evil eye ; he is of the same race, the same family. He is a bloated bladder, an empty puff, a passionate fool. I scorn him as much as I do the wearisome Iliad and the imbecile Æneid. I would not give a penny for his songs ! All for the senses, nothing for the intellect. Fie upon him, I abhor him : *he is a Greek.*" This was the highest point of the invective. He sipped from his glass of wine, and added,

"Besides, he is a jacobin."

"My good lad," then said Baylis the bookseller, a man who amused himself to put down a little the aristocracy of the Anglican architect, "your love for toryism and the high church makes you unreasonable. I have known this gentleman in his youth, I have printed his *Essay upon Revolutions*, and I assure you you are in an error."

Baylis was a Tory and a Pittite of ancient memory ;

Brown, a Whig and Foxite ; old Porden was of the high church, and partisan of George IV., for whom he had built the Chinese deformities in Brighton. M. de Chateaubriand was less offensive to Baylis than the two others ; first because Baylis had printed for him ; afterwards because the Tory bookseller loved people of the nobility.

Father Baylis then took up the defence of M. de Chateaubriand nearly in these terms :

"You understand not a word of what you say, and you reason as an old cathedral. He has not been a jacobin. He has been, as Fox and as our friend Brown here, intoxicated with the ideas of Jean Jacques, and with the philosophy of the eighteenth century. He has been of his time and country. That was his great crime ! He has lived here as a misanthropist, and been very solitary, because in his exile he was proud and unhappy; that is to say, extremely respectable."

" And by ――――," cried the artist Brown, whose soul was poetic, and whose brain was inflamed as soon as the claret circulated, "happy, happy Chateaubriand;―happy for his wandering life, miserable and misanthropical.

"In society that is sound and healthy the young people are not misanthropes, but in the cursed state of society happy he who is a misanthrope in his adolescence ! He preserves the enamel of his soul ; the down of his wing is not ruffled ; voluptuousness has not enervated him; he heeds not every wind that whistles; he folds his sail; he ardently hates the evil of this ruined world; he execrates from the depths of his soul the stigma of human slavery. At the expiration of the eighteenth century all noble spirits were doomèd; all generous hearts were ill : Napoleon, Rousseau, M. de Chateaubriand, as Goëthe, Schiller, and Byron.   After all, why reproach you, M. de Chateaubriand ?   Obermann, Rêné, Werter—fruits upon the same stalk carry the same poison.   Werter sought refuge in the tomb, Obermann amid the rocks of Fontainebleau, Rêné in the monastery, and M. de Chateaubriand fled to the wilderness.   Enthusiastic priest and apostle of Jean Jacques Rousseau, he has sought the wilds, and primitive man.   Born in the midst of the ruins of the old world, he anathematized it, then he endeavoured to reconstruct it, and he has ended by sleeping upon the broken capitol."

"Bravo!   Huzza!   Bravo the artist!   Three times three cheers for the orator!" cried Baylis.

Porden was soundly asleep.

When I had the honour, in 1829, to be introduced to M. de Chateaubriand, I was surprised to find nothing of the gloomy misanthropy and languor which the descriptions of Porden and Brown had led me to expect.   Chateaubriand was always young.   The smallness and perfection of his foot, the elegance of his contour, the carriage of his head, the grace of his movements, and beautiful intonations of his voice, will always belong to a young man.   I recollect his elastic step when at sixty years I saw him ascend a flight of steps with all the agility of a musketeer of nineteen.   This ardent champion of Christianity has always retained his vigour and

vivacity ; it is very probable that at his departure for
America he was in feeling an older man and more melancholy
than when at sixty-five he was the ornament of the Abbaye-
aux-Bois.

The whole physiognomy and figure of this great writer
was in strong relief, as were his characteristics ; his bold
outlines of feature were also marked by the graceful curve ;
his form, which was a little too small for his height, was
athletic, at the same time subtile and elastic, and seemed to
correspond with the eternal youth of his soul ; his attitudes
were dramatic, and appropriate to him ; his gray hair curled
over his full, bright, and beaming eye, and he really looked
more youthful than Benjamin Constant in his adolescence
with his flaxen hair and flowing locks.

The bright glow of hope irradiated his style ; from the
commencement of his writing, hope belonged to the man, and
never did it fail ; it carried him along through the madness
of the eighteenth century, and in the revulsions of feeling ;
it supported him in his crusade against modern philosophy.
The convert bore in his penitence the scourge for his sin.

I never knew a man who had less diplomacy or casuistry ;
who was less fitted to analyze opinions or facts. He had the
poetic and glowing style which marks the orator ; but his
genius spent itself in flights, and was never profound ; the
psychological anatomy in which Sterne, Shakspeare, and St.
Simon were skilled, was not his forte. Perhaps, with Napoleon, his is the last genius completely and intrinsically
meridional. His generosity was never cooled by calcula-

tion, nor his magnanimity abated from prudential considerations.

There was a radiance around the path of Chateaubriand, and a joyousness that was infectious ; but if the light did not always fructify, its lambent beams diffused the spirit of beauty. In such a nature we should scarcely look for the spirit of endurance or martyrdom. He was precisely the man whom the races of the North could least understand. Poor without abjectness, rich without pomp, chief of a literary sect without a code, amorous without risk to his virtue, —how shall we paint him except by contrasts ? As a natural result of this peculiar constitution, he has lost station without degradation, and attained to dignities and honours without exaltation. His nobility is in himself.

The pupil of Jean Jacques, the ardent convert to Catholicism, was evidently of high descent. His noble bearing, his step of the elasticity and firmness of the Breton, left no doubt upon that point. His enthusiasm for the doctrines of Æmilius never forsook him. In his old age it was relumined, and inspired the most brilliant pages in his work upon the state of Europe. Then people were astonished and indignant, and cried out that he had again become a liberal ; indeed, almost a republican. There was in him an extraordinary combination of antagonistic qualities. He was a democratic chevalier, a liberal loyalist, a Catholic freethinker; all in perfect sincerity.

Upon one occasion he said to me, " The old gothic chapel of St. Malo, and the beautiful gilt-edged bible of my mother, which in her hasty flight she left upon my pillow, had the largest share in my conversion." He said the truth, and these words painted him exactly. ·· With a noble soul susceptible to all beautiful impressions, with genius at the same time brilliant and melancholy, this setting sun throws her last splendours upon a decaying society.

M. de Chateaubriand belongs to the age in which he lived, with him will depart the representative of all peculiar to its greatness and virtue ; all progress is checked, all enthusiasm dies with him.

Residence in England.

CHAPTER I.

NORTHUMBERLAND.

THE first year of my residence in England, that *terra in-cognita*, passed away pleasantly, thanks to the excellent friend—then governess to the daughters of the Duke of R——, to whose care my father had confided me.   The hard manner in which I viewed the world served to render my exile more supportable ; as I saw in humanity only inbred sin, I thought that the power of enduring life must proceed from strong and manly resignation.   I was a young and brave old man, disenchanted, believing only in unhappiness, and the strength and power of resistance; a vigorous, philosophical wrestler.   I resolutely applied myself to study the languages of the North, and for pleasures I depended upon my-self—that is, upon brilliant dreams and chimeras.   The hope of returning to France when a few years should have passed, and again meeting that adored being in whom my future happiness was bound up, alone sustained me.

But when two years had thus passed, and autumn, with her cold mists and murky atmosphere, so sad in London, hovered over us, then my health suddenly failed. The elements of life were sapped by the moral struggle. The good Elizabeth, who saw my wan shadow flitting past the London streets, said to me :

" It is absolutely necessary that you should go into the country, my young friend. Set off immediately, for your illness will prove mortal here. I will give you a letter to one of my friends who lives in Northumberland, upon the borders of the ocean ; you must remain a month there, and you will recruit at the same time that you will see much to interest by its novelty. Our small maritime boroughs are very peculiar ; and surpassingly so is the one you will visit. It is not a city enriched by commerce, where amid the tumult of business we see all the luxuries which spring from civilization, but it consists of a group of about twenty huts and a church. You will perceive through all the organs of sensation your proximity to a maritime race; from the atmosphere around you draw in at every breath a strong decoction of tar and pitch, seasoned with ocean salt. You will *take* to these poor little black cabins which form the group ; some of them without windows, and half buried in mud; here and there you see one hanging from a crag; then a cluster along the sea-shore, whose foundations are of sand, and which are every day washed by the rolling waves; the only decorations are very appropriate, being fishing-nets, old baskets, fish-hooks, cords, and lines. You will be surrounded by blue jackets and red hankerchiefs, which accoutrements mark the mariner. When you have lived a week with this strong, rough race, you will find that you have fallen back five or six centuries in English life. But you will find the natives not a little amusing, I assure you, though illiterate, rough, wily, and rapacious."

The good Elizabeth was eloquent, like her sex. She had touched a chord always ready to vibrate in me—awakened a feeling always alive to the strange varieties in the human heart. I thanked her, and she put into my hands a letter for Mr. Ezekiel F——, a trader, who lived a quarter of a mile from the sea, within two gun-shots of the last hut of the borough of Berwick. She gave me also for the same person another letter from Mr. Josiah D——, a grave physician, austere in his manners, faithful in his duties, and very religious. Josiah said to his friend Ezekiel, that I selected Berwick as an economical prescription by which I could obtain the benefits of sea-bathing, without incurring the enormous expense to which those are subjected whom the physicians send to Brighton or Dover to regain the health and lighten the purse.

Elizabeth took good care to inform me that the family, who without doubt would receive me upon her recommendation, was remarkable for regularity of habits, gravity in conversation, and aversion to worldly frivolities ; that I must expect to obey the law in all its strictness ; that no light pleasures, not even intellectual, were to be met with, no *necessary superfluities* essential to the resident of a city. I enlisted as a good soldier buckles on his armour; curiosity rendered resignation easy.

The road that we travelled as we drew near to Berwick was in perfect keeping with the monotonous life I was fore-warned awaited me.   A narrow embankment to the right, and marshy plains to the left, looked dreary and desolate. As you neared the ocean, the grass looked like old straw, the yellow reeds erected their speary heads as stiff and pointed as spikes.   The vegetation resembled none I had before seen ; springing from a soil watered by the ocean, it was covered with a slimy, weedy deposit, and impregnated with saline exhalations.   The roar of the waves became intense as we approached the borough.   Towards the left, partly protected by a broken dam, a tent was pitched upon two poles, which was half draped with tattered garments and shreds of all colours.   A turf fire near the slimy and clogged entrance to the tent, served to prepare food for six or seven tattered beings, oddly attired, who prowled around it.   My travelling companions informed me that these persons were of the Gip-sey race, whom the Acts of Parliament had not yet ejected. The father, with an armful of fagots went into his tent ; a swarthy woman, half clothed, and her red eyes seeming to start from their sockets, was suckling an infant black and meagre as herself ; at a little distance stood the patriarch ancestor of this nomadic tribe, his head bald and shaking, his frame trembling with cold from the fresh sea-breezes, and his chin resting upon his naked and bleached breast.   Two little Gipsey girls, with bronzed faces but regular features, looking fierce and bold, with the leer of vice already marked in their visages, came to ask alms, which were given. The person most marked in this scene was the old grandfather, sad, solitary, and suffering; scorned without doubt by his descendants, and looked upon as a useless burden. To see him sunk in fixed and immoveable grief, you would have said that his own career of vice and misery passed in review through his mind, and at the same time the foresight of his tribe's inheritance of the same racked his soul.

We came from London, the centre of commerce, wealth, and luxury—the bazaar of Europe. Upon our route, we had seen only verdant banks, velvet lawns, cottages and villas so tastefully and charmingly adorned that they might have been mistaken for fairy palaces ;—suddenly, all this is reversed, we lose sight of cultivated nature and rural life, with all her varied attractions, and see in her place nature, the stepmother, with her gaunt figure ; she nourishes no children with kind care. Amid sterile fields and barren shores, but a few paces from fertile plains, thus is planted, almost in the midst of civilization, a savage criminal tribe ; a permanent curse, a perpetual anathema ! I remembered my Conciergerie, and comprehended that the world was not designed for enervated enjoyment, but for combat ; the body against physical evils, the soul against spiritual enemies, and the reign of sin.

I stopped at the tavern sign of *Queen Bess*, alias Elizabeth. In England, what hamlet is there, if ever so small, that has not its public house ? I never can look back to my intro-

duction to this good Queen without amusing myself at the
reminiscence ; not a feature was in place, nor were they in
harmony ; even the eyes had no connection with each other,
for the painter of the sign had put up and down, this side and
that, eyes, ears, nose, lips ; like a monk of the middle age,
who shook up the letters of a name to make an anagram.
Before announcing myself to Mr. Ezekiel F——, I thought
I would survey the coast a little. I took the path from
Queen Bess down a narrow declivity, so steep and stony it
was difficult to gain foothold, and this led to the beach. The
receding tide opened to my view an extensive beach, sparkling with mica. Behind me was the little group of huts
clustered around the parish church ; before me was the calm
sea, and in her wake sterility, but still reigned the picturesque and grand ; sharp rocks, battered by the ocean and
hollowed by the floods, assumed various bold and fantastic
forms ; upon these bleached rocks was here and there a
dwarf tree, and some marine vegetation draperied their sides,
seeming like festoons in mid air, the colours in rude and wild
contrast. There was the blue buglose, the black poppy, the
gigantic thistle, its flowers of a brilliant claret ; in short, summits the most inaccessible shone resplendent with flowers of
all colours and hues, ever varying with the touch of the powerful Artist's light and shade. Beds of marine mosses, layer
upon layer, diffused through the air their saline particles, and
the freshness of the breeze crystallizing these exhalations, led
one to imagine the rocks tapestried with a gorgeous tissue
or bespangled robe. The only buildings which were visible

from my position were the old church and alms-house (an ancient monastery transformed into an asylum for the poor); as they appeared under their garb of venerable lichens, purple, green, and blue, softened by years into different shades of gray, I felt that they had always been there, coëval with the time-honoured structures. These lichens have been thought so soft and harmonious to the eye, that many gentle men, proprietors of elegant villas, have endeavoured by art to blend the same liquid shades in the trellis work that adorns their walls ; but art cannot improvise ; it is ages that has painted them.

The wild simplicity and novelty of these views impressed my mind deeply, and filled me with delight. My health of soul and body seemed restored to me as by magic. I forgot for a moment my dangerous scepticism imbibed in my youth; those sad views of man and his destiny with which Jean Jacques, Werter, Ossian, and Lord Byron, then in the zenith of his glory, nourished the generation to which I belonged. I now felt myself renovated, and I recoiled with instinctive fear from presenting myself to my new hosts, with whose good humour I was not very favourably impressed.

I thought I would ramble about the village, and acquaint myself with the localities before being introduced to the people. In a hut of shabby appearance, sheltered by an overhanging rock, was seated a man with a wooden leg, who wore an old blue frock, the uniform custom of sailors and fishermen. He saw me approaching, and came to meet me, and proffer his services. His vocation was to point out to

4

the travellers who visited his village the various points of view along the coast; a business from which he evidently received little profit, for all the furniture in his little cabin consisted of a hammock, an old chest, a fishing line, and a telescope. This old man had been in the army, and he described to me some of the battles in which he had borne his part. By the side of his hut he had made a little garden; if one can honour by that title a space surrounded by wrecks of vessels and dilapidated boats, where a few common plants feebly thrust up their slender stalks. While he recounted to me the names of the brigs and barks of all forms and dimensions which lay at anchor; and also those of the masters whom I saw in the distance toiling in rowing that they might reach home before night, I observed a dark column of vapour, thick and heavy at its base, lighter and more elastic as it ascended upward in circles, impelled by the wind, darkening the hamlet till it reached the spot upon which we stood; this was from the ship-yard of the place, where the planks were bent by means of smoke. Occupations, pleasures, pains, remembrances, toils, all spoke of the struggle of man against nature; all was connected with the ocean, that sleeping giant. I requested the man to show me the way to the house of Mr. Ezekiel F——. We again passed Queen Bess, and stopped before a lonely brick house, in which we could neither see lights nor any one moving.

CHAPTER II.

I KNOCKED a long time, and found it difficult to gain admittance. The inmates were all asleep in this regular house. A large woman was at length aroused; she came to the window in a brown robe, holding the strings of her bunting cap in her hand, and after having questioned me through the window, she proceeded to remove sundry bars and unlock padlocks, which secured all the avenues, and then, after admitting me, barring and locking as carefully again. She told me that the family were asleep, and that I should deliver my letter to Mr. Ezekiel the next morning, and she would prepare me a bed. In passing along I observed that the house resembled a secular monastery. The tone of the servant, one of those women, all bone and muscle, like Sir Walter Scott's Meg Merrilies, was indescribably solemn and lugubrious. But habituated to English ideas, which, in 1818 at least yielded free scope to all peculiarities and individualities of character,—warned, besides, through Mr. Josiah D——,—the aspect around did not much disturb me, and I slept peaceably, waiting till the sun should throw light upon this family of the ancient world transplanted into the new.

I was then far from precisely divining the origin of manners so peculiar; but the enigma has been since solved. I will here throw out some remarks upon the peculiar character of the English, much decried, but little understood. The most marked characteristic in the Anglo-Saxon race is worship of the past. This savour of antiquity emanates from their insular position, redolent of charms for the imagination; but is attended with real dangers and also benefits. We witness among them, apparently without alteration, old laws and customs. That gothic and shapeless tower of Babel, which the English call their jurisprudence, only supports itself from its antiquity. The barbarity of their legal code is contrary, thanks to the age, to their national good sense, which corrects it in the practice. The country gentleman of 1818 still recalls to your mind, by his habits and costume, Sir Roger de Coverley, the hero of Addison. Thus the city Quaker is the living type of the times of William Penn. In the vicinity of Whitechapel, the eastern extremity of London, you will encounter some colonies of Anabaptists, who, however little to your taste, insist upon you following them to their lofts, where they *hold meetings*, and some Boanerges, eloquent as John of Leyden, holds forth, and anathematizes the Amale-kites. From traditions of the past, which live in the present, proceeds that originality of character, which offers so various and rich material for the pencil of the novelist and eye of the observer. You must mingle with the aristocracy of. England to see the highest polish and most exquisite refine-ment of manners ; but the originality vanishes as the sharp points are filed away—the individuality which distinguishes one man from another. If, as Diderot, you prefer the strong impress of character, native and rude, "to the uniform roundness of the polished pebbles, heaved upon the strand by the rolling billows, and polished by the attrition," visit Wales, the Orkneys, and Scotland; there you will reap an ample harvest of the humorous and grotesque,—of living antiquities ; you will see notions sanctioned as time-honoured customs, and religious rites adored.*

Here, for example, enclosed within these brick walls to which chance directed me, where I slept for the first time in a little village scarcely inscribed upon the map, lived at the commencement of the nineteenth century, and perhaps still lives, one of the most curious remnants of ancient Europe that could be imagined. He was a wreck, well preserved, of that ancient and formidable race of Calvinistic *Covenanters*, who counted as many martyrs as executioners ; who made England what she is, a nation harsh, haughty, taciturn ; austere when possessed of power ; exalted in seasons of persecution ; as implacable in their resentments as constant in attachments ; retaining for a hundred and fifty years their rancour against that feeble, romantic, and unhappy monarch whom they beheaded ; and consecrating their martyrs to worship till time shall be no more. This people is unswerving in probity, unalterable in feeling, undying in recollections of the past. They marry their children only in their own ranks, and grant the *Philistines* neither son nor daughter ; praying

---

* The foregoing remarks become less applicable every day to Young England.

to St. Cromwell every day in their secret oratory ; all ready to *fight the good fight* ; bewailing constantly with grief which is not without hope, the good days when the Saints and the Elect ruled the land.

In this primitive family I had become a resident.   The head, Ezekiel F——, whose Biblical name announced his descent, a trader and Calvinist, was a man of forty.   He followed the business of his ancestors, selling grain, hops, and coal ; he was renowned for his probity, and was rich, temperate, calm, and inexorable ; his character was stamped upon his rigid and immoveable features.   His six feet of height, which seemed to augment from his slow, solemn step and unbending form, with lips compressed, brow serious ; as soon as you had seen him once you had seen him always ; he would remain for ever engraved in your memory.   The Biblical regicides in their long parliament must have borne this physiognomy. His Old Testament phraseology and austere manner, never relaxing, completed his resemblance, or rather identity, with the signers of the famous *Covenant.*   I do not remember during the two months that I was an inmate in his house, hearing Ezekiel F—— pronounce an indiscreet word or unpremeditated phrase ; not a sign or gesture ever betrayed an emotion, or the least gaiety of spirit.   He spoke little, and every one yielded prompt obedience to an order uttered in his grave tone with austere mien.   No subject was discussed in his presence.   I have seen him do a kind act without emotion, and show severity to extreme rigour without testifying any regret.   He was a patriarch of the ancient law in all its rigour, and, it must be added, in all its power and grandeur.

The pharisaical precision, the undeviating system, which guided the movements of this family, did not encourage me to expect the warm and glowing welcome with which the people of the South greet their guests. But, in recompense, there was a certain delicacy in my host's attention, generous and urbane, though antique in its demonstration, that left me at liberty to pursue my own path, and that proved by acts, not expressions, his benign watchfulness ; this moved me from one of a tribe so austere. I believed I could not better evince my gratitude than by conforming as far as possible to the rules of the house, which in the mean time were not imposed.

The family rose at five through all seasons. An hour was passed in prayer afterwards; but from this rite my title of foreigner permitted me to abstain; there followed a low, monotonous murmuring of some old rhymes consecrated by the ancient sufferings of the party, and to which the profoundness of conviction imparted a certain energy and grandeur. At eight, at two, and at seven, the large walnut table, blackened by age, but without tablecloth, was covered with healthy aliments, abundant, though scarcely ever varied. From garret to cellar there was not an article of mahogany to be seen, not a trace of the precious metals, nor of the pleasing and brilliant ornaments which usually embellish the dwellings of the rich; all was of dark polished oak and walnut; several immense chairs, six feet high, straight and polished backs, with low wooden bottoms, suitable for an oratory* upon occasion; one solitary clock, a very useless piece of machinery where habit alone served for clepsydra and dial; these, with the large table before mentioned, were the furniture of the hall or parlour, the walls of which were covered with paper of a solemn gray, without figures or border: in fine, all the abominations of the Egyptians were banished with a severity unknown even to the Quakers. But the utmost care was evident in the arrangement of the waxed and polished furniture; there was the luxury of neatness, but withal a sort of solemn order, which left a mournful impression upon the beholder. At the end of the parlour there were some brown wooden shelves within the wall, symmetrically placed, which served for the tea equipage of Wedgewood ware. My eyes frequently turned towards this precious recess, it being the only ornament of the dwelling.

I had been about eight days in the house, when, after the dinner at two o'clock, Ezekiel F——, seeing my eyes fixed upon these shelves, which displayed traces of the only worldly luxury that my host permitted himself and his family to indulge in, took my hand, and led me with a mysterious air towards the object of my involuntary attention; he then removed a tea-pot from a wooden tray, and showed me the reverse side, and, what was my surprise! I saw upon the black ground of this tray a magnificent portrait of Cromwell. You had the man, full length, square built, powerful, hilarious, resolute, the always present idol of

---

* In French, " prie-Dieu."

this house: here was that ardent and powerful head which made his country the queen of Protestantism and the North. He was represented as standing, his hand·upon the mace, the eyebrow shaggy and frowning, the upper lip prominent, seeming half moved to merriment—such as the bold Protector of England showed himself, when, with tears in his eyes, and the name of the Most High in his mouth and heart, armed with his short sword, he thrust aside the crafty and imbecile crowd who knelt before him, and took possession of the keys of Parliament.

A grave smile gleamed through the dark features of Ezekiel, that I had never seen illumined before: the tray retook its position, the tea-pot its stand; all returned to the accustomed silence. See we not here some shadowy and remote recurrence of extinguished glory. With the children of the old familiar saint, with these Trappists of Calvinism, there is a conviction which attaches itself to Moses, that if their generation subsists, it is to reign in the Millennium.

Here was revived the old Bible of Esdras. All the members of the family were overshadowed by the priest and patriarch; to them his words were laws; upon him all was modulated. Mrs. Sarah F———, " his companion before the Lord"—thus he called her—was silent when he was present; but in his absence she held the reins of government. A liberal charity to the poor, judiciously distributed, and economy without avarice, distinguished them both. A son, removed in the fulness of manhood, left to the care of his father a young widow with three children, all of tender age.

4*

Ruth—the name of the Puritan widow—had only two thoughts, to pray to the Lord, and to bring up her children. Hers was a beauty pale and fair; her blood circulated slowly, without impulsion or warmth; she had always been holy from temperament and taste.*

The daughter, Sybilla, with brown complexion and blue eyes, owed to habit and education the devout and precise manner constantly inculcated by her father.† Nature had not so formed her. Beneath this demure look, pensive and solemn, a fearful ardour and intensity of soul was sometimes betrayed. A sudden motion, a flash, a furtive glance, would unconsciously speak of feeling repressed, vivacity subdued. Subjected to this factitious routine of life, she had yielded not as to tyranny, but as to law. She had no suspicion that there was any thing else in life than the care of the household and piety. This untoward struggle between natural feeling and the restraint imposed by education, was most evident when a young man of the same cast came to visit the family. Formalist, as all his sect, he dressed throughout the year in brown barrican. Owing to the moderation and sobriety of his life, his complexion retained the brilliant freshness of boyhood; he wore a hat whose broad brim extended five inches in width, overshadowing his fine face, covering a forest of dark, rich, clustering locks, and concealing an eye

---

* A very inadequate idea of a holy character.—TRANSLATOR.

† We see here, in two passages, that the author uses the word devout as ceremonial in this clause.

which awed you from its calmness and depth. He was a youthful Hampden.

It was not difficult for me to penetrate the views of young Abraham, or see behind the veil of Sybilla's heart; and it was pleasant and touching to watch the development of their loves: grave, sedate, without any discordant note, any pique and reconciliation following; unattended by the sigh of the lover, or any coquetry of the mistress. Certainly a half-comical feeling came over me in observing a courtship in which the lover resembled a confessor, and the beloved a penitent. Nothing, however, is so serious as true passion, and Abraham and Sybilla so evidently existed for and in each other, their pure, grave love, never unconscious of the presence of the Most High, resembling Eternity in its depth and calm, affected me deeply. I was softened even to tears when Sybilla said to Abraham once in parting with him: " May the Lord be with you !" Abraham replied: " And you, my beloved, may you dwell under the shadow of His wings."

CHAPTER III.

THE contrast of this foreign people, so vigorous and chaste,
though their habits, no doubt, were formed from erro-
neous doctrines, but which accorded so well with the manly
hearts of the English, and the elevation of their society,
brought forcibly to my view the emptiness of that scepticism
so rife in my own country. But I suffered deeply in seeing how
exclusive such a people become; how stern and hard in their
sincerity.   A sadness came over me; I felt myself isolated as
a stranger who spills the salt under an Arabian's hospitable
tent.   I found protection and an asylum, but not that fraternity of feeling, that sympathy which doubles life, and without which all is solitude.   I felt humiliated for my race.*
Nothing could give me the remembrances, the regrets, the
doctrines of my hosts: we were united through benevolence
and gratitude, but not by community of ideas; thus they
could yield me without a feeling of deprivation to visit other
inhabitants of the borough.

The people here gained their livelihood by the sea, and
knew no other element; her they ploughed, and from her they
reaped their harvest; they even gathered her wrecks.   They

---

* Meaning the French or Celtic.

were sailors, fishermen, corsairs, cordwainers, smugglers, and receivers of stolen goods. If a ship stranded, it was a windfall. Then the men unloaded their boats, and dragged them along the putrid marshy fen, where the efforts of beasts of burden could not gain footing; they mended the keel of a vessel that the winds and waves had split, and for this purpose they piled heaps of peat and coke on the shore, the only native riches of their soil. The corsair lived in a little cabin built upon a crag, which seemed suspended in mid air. Behind this projecting rock were moored the Holland pinnaces, freighted with contraband goods : it is across these thorny bristly reeds and rushes, over putrid marshes, that the horses fly with their illicit charge. When the weather is stormy, you will see men passing down the bleached reefs, and remain watching for hours, concealed between the spiked and thorny weeds, covered with foam, waiting till the ocean shall heave up men and riches. They have perceived from a distance a ship in distress ; they demand from the floods a part of the prey. If the sea heaves up the body of an English mariner, they despoil, and if there are remains of life, frequently despatch him, looking with care all around, from fear that another marauder may come to share their booty. It was upon a shore as desolate, peopled with inhabitants as savage, that an English poet, Lillo—who had some flashes of genius—has laid the scene that he has painted with all the horrors of reality. A fisherman and his wife, hunting for prey, find a sailor who still lives, and they cut his throat that they may despoil him:

they afterwards recognise in the corpse a long-lost and idolized son, the only hope of their miserable and criminal old age.

But the sea, which witnessed so many daring exploits, and brought our men so many wrecks, would sometimes prove to them a devouring element; frequently in her gradual encroachments she would sweep off the poor fisherman, his cabin, with the sandbank upon which he built. Such is this horde among whom I domiciled: adventurous men without ambition, courageous without any aspirations for glory, ferocious without remorse. And King George IV. was their king; London was the metropolis of their country. Who would be astonished, then, should they worm themselves to London and Paris?

As to the notables of the place, besides Mr. Ezekiel F——, whom I have described already, I will specify the attorney, famous for rapacity; the mayor, who exemplified a rotundity worthy of his station, whose dress was a brown coat, bordered with silver lace two inches in width; then there was the young vicar, a gentle and pleasing person, who bitterly lamented his hard fate in being exiled upon these inhospitable shores; in fine, the rector, an old Oxford student, an excellent Hellenist, whose exemplary industry and virtues obtained the reward of this miserable curacy. His only revenue, the tithes, was a mockery of the law, for the soil was either rocky or entangled with rushes, or a barren sandy shore, upon which would grow neither grain, vines, nor fruit. I pitied this poor and honest priest, with his four daughters, beautiful and lovely; he was always occupied in resisting the aggression and opposition from discontented purveyors, or in calming the attorney, who was the terror of the village. The unhappy man was sixty-five years old, and his dream of glory still supported him. With the rush-light* prepared in the dilapidated manse, which he used for economy, much as its flickering flame wearied his old eyes, he laboured over his notes *Bibliothèque de Photius;* learned notes that he compelled me to read. If this modest minister had received pecuniary aid, perhaps England might have claimed a second Bentley.

I admired sea views, but the intrinsic charm of the ocean, with her ever varied spectacles, which was attraction enough in itself, the taciturnity of my hosts, the duties and the labours of the two ministers, would have sent me to her shores as a resource in the deficiency of society. The description of ocean scenery, and all the dramatic and heart-stirring scenes of life intermingled with her waves, has gained poetical renown for a large part of the great English writers—witness Thomson, who has reproduced them with an exuberance which is quite dazzling ; Crabbe, who has delineated them with the minutiæ of a Dutch marine painter ; Byron, who writes with haughty disdain of man, but at home upon the ocean, has upon this theme shown a concentration and depth of thought and feeling, a brilliancy of colouring like the radiating sunbeams which form the crystal in her depths. Southey, also, in language as exuberant as her swelling floods, has gained

---

* The poorer classes in England make use of this economical light.

entrance into our heart of hearts.   But the reality is more ideal than the ideal of the artist.   How often, in a fisherman's cabin, the sea calm, have I watched its waves; slowly her vast bosom heaves as if from emotion ; then a wave, swelling as it rolls ; then another and another, which, dying, retreat in silence, floating lightly in the midst of universal repose.   Then from afar I would hear the almost imperceptible sound of a breaker, lashing lightly, as if in sport, the flanks of some bark at anchor. .

After the retreat of the tide, the golden beach displayed the treasures of the sea, deposited by the waves ; the medusæ, a species of gelid substance, which glitters under the water like pearls, have an exquisite beauty in their ever-varied forms, and are more delicate than the work of a jewel-ler ; the sertullaria, a plant which respires, an animal that vegetates—a paradox of nature, and a chain between the animate and inanimate.   From the knotty stalk and branches of this animated tree, one sees through the transparent vesi-cles numerous little talons elongating themselves to find their prey.

My youthful literature, even the study of Byron, tended to conceal the Most High from me, by calumniating his creatures.   Like all my contemporaries, I had hearkened by turns to the Wertherian wail of despair, and utilitarian theory which began to invade Europe.   In my musings along the sea-shore, I revolted against the incomplete theism of Rous-seau, the sceptical raillery of Voltaire, the pantheistic hypo-theses of the Germans, and the mechanism of Bentham.—

"Yes," said I to myself, "the Glorious, the Beautiful exists; supreme and divine beauty is superior to the useful ; it contains and surpasses it. The beauty lavished upon creation attests the ideal ; the glory of nature independent of the useful." Thus the religious idea which had been undeveloped in childhood from adverse influences, arose in my heart as a new source of life.

Frequently, in the warmest days, I saw myriads of phosphorescent points, wafted upon the marine mosses. I amused myself by gathering them in the palm of my hand, and letting them escape in a visible flame. I continued my walks even through fogs and tempests. There is something singularly picturesque in the undefined forms of the ships at anchor, as seen through the mist ; and the cries of the sailors, with the noise of the floods, which you cannot see through the haze, increase the effect. Perhaps the weather is decidedly tempestuous, the scene upon the coast, grand or beautiful as it may be, becomes wildly sublime ; all the sea-birds, in screaming, announce the tempest, as they wheel around in a cloud, then hover over the sea and raze the foaming billows ; battalions of wild ducks mount up the sky, higher than gun can reach. From all points of the village men descend to the shore in their frocks, with their hooks and grappling irons. The women, almost all fair and pretty, throw the skirts of their gowns over their heads, as a handkerchief, and they follow on. I have seen the men of the village resist the entreaties of their wives, mothers, and loved ones, and, notwithstanding their innate rapacity, brave all the terrors of the tempest, that they may save some fellow-creature in distress.   The night before, these same men rifled without mercy a poor Holland sloop, and threw into the sea the wretched sailors.   Religion and crime, pity and barbarity, were confounded in an inextricable maze—such is man! It was then that I comprehended Shakspeare for the first time; I had read him with the eyes alone— I now read him with the understanding.   I re-read his Macbeth, and I discovered that the basis of his power lay in his profound knowledge of mankind.   Here was my initiation also in Tacitus and Thucydides, whom I never forsook.

A mile from the village is an islet of rocks, on which is built a Pharos, or lighthouse.*   The ocean waves lash it in their fury, but cannot prevail against it—for it is founded upon a rock.   This giant of the ocean, with flaming eyes, is always upon guard, lighting the recesses of the deep ; and it is a sublime spectacle in a storm to see the waves besieging this citadel, lashing her sides, ascending her tower up the shelving rocks, inaccessible to human foot, all to no purpose ; then, as the waves heave, the living light reveals the yawning caves of the ocean, opening tombs, ready to swallow man and his frail barks.

Notwithstanding my frequent absences, my good hosts, the Puritans, satisfied with my punctual attendance at the hours of repast, had, I thought, as much friendship for me as their faith and habits would allow them to feel or express.   My regularity of life seemed to them remarkable in a Frenchman.

---

* The South Stack lighthouse.

Abraham had received the confession of Sybilla, with the approbation of her father ; calm felicity, with its soft halo, shed its beams over this house. The day for the nuptials was fixed, and I anticipated much pleasure from sharing in these interesting rites.

Suddenly I heard that the good Elizabeth was ill, three miles from London, and that her life was despaired of. I immediately bid farewell to my hosts, though I acknowledge I quitted with pain this strange household, where I had seen all the virtues flourish, under the most ferocious dogmas, professed with zeal by these innocent souls. I left the lovers upon the point of being united, and the father of the family, with the old mother, in the possession of moderate joy ; in the mean time they seemed sad in losing their guest. Ezekiel, who had not yet pretended to convert me, and had never *held forth*, (as the Independents express themselves,) that is to say, expounded his doctrines to save me from the Moabites, could not prevent himself from saying to me, as he pressed my hand in parting, that "The world was the furnace into which Korah, Dathan, and Abiram had fallen ; so, if I obtained not divine grace, I should consume in the flames of the world : I must remember the Lord ; in that case his house should always prove to me the Ark of Noah, in which I should repose without fear." These words, sincere and grave, drawn forth by paternal interest, without a taint of affectation or commonplace civility, affected me strangely.

CHAPTER IV.

I HAD the joy to find dear Elizabeth convalescent. After two years passed in London and Scotland, I felt strongly drawn to the little hamlet upon the rocks, to the Puritan family, the portrait of Cromwell beneath the tea-pot, and to my ancient English rector, unique specimen of the old English type, which would require the pen of Richter, the pencil of Goya, or the crayon of Charlet, to describe the mixture of quaintness, shrewdness, and simplicity which characterized him.   Upon my arrival, instead of repairing first to the beach, as at my first visit, I hastened to Ezekiel's mansion.

It was early in the afternoon when I reached Ezekiel's door, where I knocked a long time in vain for admittance ; I could rouse no one; all seemed dead in the house.   Astonished, alarmed, I hastened to the hut of the fisherman, who had before piloted me upon these shores.   I found him occupied in repairing some old nets ; for the dampness of his sorry abode had made him almost blind.   I asked him after Ezekiel and family, whose house seemed deserted.

"Ah ! sir," said the old man, " *God has dealt rudely with them.** If you will come with me you shall see their old ser-

---

* This was his literal reply.

vant, Rachel Blount, who lives yonder in that cabin. She will tell you their whole story, which she knows better than I do, for she has lived with them. She tells the story, weeping, every day."

I followed him to the dwelling of Rachel Blount—the servant who opened the door for me the evening of my first visit. She knew me, and after the first greetings, she gave me the following account :—

"Two days after you left us, the marriage of Miss Sybilla to the godly young man, Abraham S——, was to take place; but God in his anger visited the crimes of men : *he* had otherwise decreed ; and the next morning all was ended—there was no more happiness for that family. Sad news spread from village to village and reached ours ; there was a war with the United States, and the press-gang scoured the country, seizing as they went along all the young, the middle-aged, and even old men.

'Master Abraham walked with Miss Sybilla along the beach on the wedding morning. We followed shortly, without being able to overtake them, for the brigands seized Abraham, sir ; Oh ! the enemies of God, to seize that innocent lamb from the arms of the young girl. They dragged him away with them, the cruel creatures ! notwithstanding the lovers begged that the marriage might first take place. But they refused ; for the glory and joy of such wretches is to break the hearts of families. Master Abraham was handcuffed as a robber and carried off in triumph, the wretches shouting and singing as they went along, leaving the father,

mother, and young girl to bewail their misery.   The next
morning when the vessel was to sail,——oh ! was there not
weeping and wailing in our village ?   All the sons, the wives,
the daughters, the fathers, stood upon the beach ; and their
farewell screams were not heard ; the mothers knelt upon
the wet sand, and stretched out their arms towards their
children, imploring that they might be allowed to embrace
them once more !   Not a permission granted—not a farewell—not a last look !   We could easily perceive the people
upon the deck, but could distinguish no one.   Oh, the Moabites ! oh, the cursed !   What barbarity !"

The old woman wiped her tears and continued, with her
plain good sense, pathetic and simple : "Oh ! sir, what a
horrible business is this impressment !*   Is it not an abomination before God ?   It is said that all this is necessary; how
can that be ?   Necessary to send demons with firearms to
rend asunder the true love and honest pleasures God has
given us in our huts.   If they had delayed one week, or one
day only, my young mistress would still be living.   Every
body confesses that this impressment is unjust, wicked, detestable ; and for sixty years, since I have had the use of my
reason, I have seen it practised in every war.   Why is it,
sir ?   Is it because men have not the fear of God before their
eyes, nor love of each other in their hearts ?"

The old woman continued her narrative : "Abraham went

---

* The laws concerning impressment have been revised since the time
here referred to by Chasles.

with his companions in misfortune, and Sybilla heard that the young man died on the passage. From that time she was never seen to smile ; her head became weak, she spoke low, and talked to herself ; she was always very gentle, patiently supported life, and still prayed, but she was not herself. Then, sir, came the fatal mistake of her father: seeing his daughter survive her affliction, and advance in age, he determined she should marry. She gently refused, and all the family supplicated Ezekiel to leave the unhappy girl in peace; but he answered: ' The sacred law had ordained it: *Increase and multiply*, said the Lord.' *Ezekiel* willed it; and a preacher of righteousness was selected for a husband for Sybilla, and the day fixed for the wedding. Then, sir, she resisted no longer. Since the departure of Abraham, her mind had never been settled, and during one stormy night, three days before that fixed for the wedding, she threw herself from a rock into the sea.

"The body floated upon the beach, and was found covered with black moss. Desolation and despair! Her mother soon died; and her father, who said the hand of God was upon him, shut himself up in his house, and has not been out since. There he lives in misery and wretchedness, reaping the bitter fruits he has sown. He has sent me away, me, his faithful servant; and I think, sir, he will die without opening the door at which you knocked in vain."

This is the second impressive lesson in my early life. A lesson more powerful than any learned from books has reached me from this humble maritime hamlet,—precious wreck of past time.   I became conscious of the deep interest which attaches to human life, whether clothed in regal robes or the shreds of poverty.   The shades of character and details of ordinary life, which are only despised for want of observation, I learned to appreciate; and I gained more knowledge of man from attending to them than I could from the highest speculations.   In fact, generalities and abstractions deceive us; the vast horizon effaces contours and confounds objects; in widening the range of vision all hues are blended and no forms are definite.   From hence arises the monotony of history; also the disappointment we experience from reading the narratives of travellers, who too frequently forget that the charm and soul of life consists in its infinite variety.

From this period I have felt a horror and detestation of every thing false and exaggerated, and this feeling is always on the increase.   Instead of the theatrical and factitious, I have witnessed in this hamlet the most sublime views the world can offer—the majesty of nature, truth of passion, and depth of faith.

English Society in 1817.

CHAPTER I.

SOME TYPES.

WHEN I returned to London from the solitary shores of Northumberland—to the rush and tide of life in a great city—a new world opened upon my view, with which in my two years' secluded life I had not commingled. I now mixed in the society of London, which was at the same time frivolous and grave; I joined her fêtes, and witnessed her ambitions and luxuries. I now tasted for the first time—thanks to my charming meditative retirement when worn and wearied by the bustle and noise of the city—the ardent pleasure of studying man in this panorama of human life; I also gained my Shaksperian education, which ever after dwelt in the depths of my soul. But a peculiar melancholy, stern in judgment, gentle in demeanour, has never been dissipated by time.

At this period I saw the most celebrated characters of the day; stars, as they were styled; I also became acquainted

5

types of political and fashionable society—which last are a mixture of wild liberty and narrow convention; but I feel no right to distinguish these by name.

One of these types was the Baronet, a tory, and supporter of the ancient constitution, a man who speculatively detested corruption, but his mind was infected with pernicious prejudices; six times in his life he had paid five thousand pounds sterling for his seat in parliament; besides his assumption of unimpeachable integrity, he lays claim to unbounded charity and mercy, which he has testified by causing the transportation to Botany Bay of the starving wretch who stole a hare from his premises.

I also became acquainted with an ancient radical, a disciple of Godwin's. His grand refrain was America! his factotum Cobbett ; he thought that a government without imposts was perfection, and the highest political attainment was to hire a cheap president, and obtain food at a low rate.

His son was a modern radical; he stopped not at such material advantages, but his stand-point was principles: he had a theory of government cut and dried to suit all nations and ages; "he reasoned according to the nature of things" —this was his stereotyped expression. He governed by axioms; society was a piece of mechanism, never out of time or tune. By force of syllogism and excessive clearness he succeeded in making himself unintelligible; by strength of logic he put to flight common sense; from the excess of his philanthropy he sympathized with no one. When his daughter eloped with a captain of dragoons, the father put this clause in his advertisement of the case: "If the young girl refuses to return to her inconsolable parents, she is desired at least to send back the little key of the chest of linen she has carried off." I have known him to visit an asylum for the insane, and argue with the inmates to prove to them that it is very unreasonable to be crazy.   Oh, these men of rules and measures, axioms and syllogisms; the grand philosophical reformers!   I have also become somewhat skilled in dandyism, from inspection of the English type. The marks are, an ineffable scorn for his species, whom the dandy spares no pains to insult.   He jostles aside all men and women who encumber his path, makes a great display of his linen, moves about as a puppet, and from fifteen even till sixty no smiles or tears furrow his smooth visage; nevertheless there are visible divers strange grimaces, like *his* type, the monkey.

But among the most distinguished in London circles was the rich merchant, the man of wealth, *par excellence*,—aye, honest in the midst of his temptations, for he does not wait to be dunned for payment of his notes; he commits no sins but such as are *venial*, and easily pardoned; he only oppresses the weak, and never compromises himself.   He is renowned for his virtues, of which fortitude must be chief, for he has seen his ancient fellow-student and friend die of hunger without wincing.   This last type is common and inevitable in a commercial community.

After discovering the springs which move these types, whether the politician, dandy, or merchant, you are soon wearied. I felt myself more attracted towards the eccentricities of the day; men strong in their individuality: Bentham, Coleridge, Southey, Ugo Foscolo, Wordsworth, all of whom I heard disparaged, which proved to me their worth. My extreme youth enabled me to enjoy the peculiar pleasure of observers—that is, of remaining unnoticed in my corner, and hearing and seeing without disturbing the current. Of those powerful and active elements of society the trace is half effaced.

With all the polish and splendour of the English aristocracy, there is a certain monkish restraint pervades their circles ; indeed, the structure of English society is an anomaly; even in their pleasures they are regulated by rules as arbitrary as in their business; society is subjected to a wearisome slavery to ceremony and etiquette, even to fantastic forms of the mode: thus officers and peers of the realm imprison themselves in steel corsets. With this universal vassalage to conventions, and the attendant monotony, they are also characterised by fierce pride, license in morals, and freedom from restraints of law. There are women in high life who disdain not to enter into the arena of pamphleteer warfare to punish a faithless lover, or avenge their own honour. Such was the character of the people among whom I had now come to reside.

This was the state of society that Lord Byron attacked so virulently. The noble ladies whom he disparaged, and whom he, despising their soirées, quitted for the woods and shores of the Hellespont, repaid his satires with usury. But the incense offered at his shrine had been great as the hatred he inspired.

Afterwards, as if in defiance of scorn, he became a disciple of Brummel; he was initiated by his admirers into the secrets of dandyism, with all its assumptions and puerile haughtinesses; he received from them the baptism of the caste: and this hero, satirist, philosopher, and god of song, never lost this frivolous taint, so unnaturally allied with the tragic grandeur to which he aspired.

In the saloons which I frequented, the talk was of the satanic dandy who lived upon dry bread through fear of becoming corpulent, and who was weighed every day to assure himself that he had not. He affected the *roué*, and numerous singular manias; then, sick at heart, he shut himself up in his library, seeking for some true emotion in contrast with his heartless dissipation.

It is true that among the fellow-citizens and contemporaries of Byron the most simple were possessed with fancies scarcely less strange than were his. Some were zealous and fanatical, as Montgomery and the Reverend Edward Irving, anathematizing unmercifully all the ungodly; others, as the ancient Godwin, professed a philosophical latitude in morals, even to the annulling of marriage. The friends of the good Elizabeth, whom I met at her house, belonged to the rigid class of religionists; a Calvinist herself, and inclining towards Methodism, she had no connection with the Benthams, the Hazlitts, Cobbets, Hunts, and all that stirring race who are the representatives of the great idea, the perfectibility of man ; therefore, seeing England only under her guidance and auspices, one important phase of her society would have remained concealed from my view but for a little circumstance which I will relate.

In the most stormy days of the French Revolution my father became intimate with an able English lithographer, who was an old friend of Fox, and, like most of the artists, a determined radical. It was through this person, Thomas Brown, that I became versed in the extraordinary phenomena of English parties: extreme Whiggism, the American republicanism, and the utilitarian school. The leaders of these parties, to whom I was introduced, did not feel embarrassed by my presence, a lad without pretensions, of whom, besides, they might make a convert. My tendency was not sceptical, but in silence of the spirit I hearkened and deliberated : I adored truth, but I did not believe she would unveil her face at the first summons. By what right could my modesty be called scepticism ? Do we assay the gold because we doubt its presence ? When will man cease to divide mankind into two classes, the credulous and the incredulous ?

CHAPTER II

FOSCOLO.

THOMAS BROWN, whom methinks I still see, in his deep yellow vest, to the cut and colour, alias Fox, his shirt frill displaying some rents, so did Fox's; his nose a little too red, an unfortunate likeness there; and his boot-tops upon the model of his political rival; he was the medium of my introduction to the Corypheuses of the parties, sometimes at a club, sometimes at the houses of his friends, as the case might be. Through his good offices I became acquainted with Cobbett, Hunt, Sir Francis Burdett, Bentham, and even that radical Italian, the lion of the age, Ugo Foscolo, who played the eccentric part in London that Byron did in Italy. He was possessed with the fancy of erecting a Grecian temple for his private dwelling-house; and this, which was characteristic of the artist and poet, he expected to pay for by his books and articles in reviews.

In 1819 I was first introduced to Foscolo. All the decorations of his house were pagan. He had an Apollo in his boudoir and a Jupiter in his ante-chamber; a little portable altar served him for a stove; and I am sure he lamented that he must wear the modern costume. His flaming eyes, tangled tresses, the curule chair which was his throne, more-

over the maledictions which he hurled against his enemies in
every word he uttered, caused him to be to me an object of
astonishment rather than interest.   He spared not any whom
he considered his political or poetical enemies.   I believed I
saw an exaggeration of Alfieri, who was himself an exaggeration of Dante.   He did not talk, he declaimed: he read not,
but shouted.   He was more theatrical than the theatre.   In
the mean time this was not affectation; his mad vehemence
had become habitual to him.

One may say that Foscolo inherited democracy from his
ancestors, and that he was born a fiery democrat.   According to tradition his family line dated back to the sixth century, when a number of fugitive tribes sought refuge among
the lagoons of the Adriatic, and there founded the Republic
of St. Mark.   Foscolo, descended from one of those fugitive
families, was born at Zante, between 1772 and 1776,* he
was reared from infancy upon the glory of his ancestors, and
inspired it with every breath.   Still very young, he drew
upon himself, from the temerity of his language, the Argus
eyes of the State Inquisition, which even to the last agony
preserved its terrible power.   Summoned before the inquis-
itors, he repaired to the tribunal, and his mother from the
threshold of the door, called to him, " Go, my son, and die
sooner than dishonour thyself by betraying thy friends."
The son was worthy of such a mother; his whole life resounded with the echo of these Spartan words.

---

* The date of his birth is uncertain; Foscolo has indicated, by turns,
1772, '75, and '76, as epochs of his birth.

Venetian liberty fell, as is well known, under the blows of Austria; the young Foscolo quitted his country for Milan; and there he became acquainted with the amiable Parini. His education, which was commenced at Venice, continued at Malta, aided by Parini, and was completed at the university of Padua. He returned afterwards and passed some weeks at Venice, and then travelled through Tuscany and other parts of Italy. He was never intimate with Alfieri; the resemblance was too prominent for intimacy; it is not from similitude, but contrast, that friendship ensues. Foscolo could retain no friends, for he could pardon no error. The eccentricities which early separated him from his contemporaries, surrounded him with enemies to the end of his career.

He was appointed secretary to the embassy which the republic of Venice sent to Napoleon; he then saw the liberty of Venice bought and sold as a bale of goods; the admiration that he had felt for France and her chief turned to scorn. He left Venice, now become an Austrian province, and went to reside in that part of Italy which was then called the Cis-Alpine republic.

There, goaded by indignation and deep despair, he gave utterance to those feelings in Jacobi Ortis—an extraordinary work of truth and exaggeration, of declamatory rhetoric and sincere eloquence. It is lofty in language, but poor in thought. Reminiscences of ancient tragedy, imitations of the Eloise and Werter, are confounded in this work, which is a fac-simile of the civilization of the south of Europe—a zone

5*

which has been in decadence since two hundred years; these letters, with their efforts to express pathos, passion, and sublimity, resulting in—nothing, or for the most but in epithets, or pomp and harmony of language, betray the last aspirations of a people sensitive rather than sensible.   The *Letters of Jacobi Ortis*, in their fragmentary style and vehement expression, produced an extraordinary sensation.   Such gigantic patriotism struck all imaginations; Foscolo had transformed political ideas into passionate poetry.   Shortly after this he joined the Italian legion, commanded by French generals. Poet and warrior, he took part in the defence of Genoa, which brought so much honour to Massena.   Under the fire of the enemy's batteries, in the midst of the tumult of a siege, his poetical talents were developed and his learning manifested.   This was the beautiful epoch of his life.   His noble odes, addressed to Louise Pallavicini, were composed at Genoa; and a short time after his commentary upon the poem of Catulle was published in the same city.   Italian literature offers few elegiac gems comparable to the odes we have cited; a classic grace respires in every word.   The commentary is a singular parody; a combination of erudition and mad folly, a wild extravagance which the lyric permits her votaries to indulge in.

Foscolo, who licensed himself in invectives, expressed without let or hindrance his scorn for three or four editions of a journal published at Milan.   *Ajax*, a tragedy of Foscolo's, furnished them an opportunity for avenging themselves.   The tragedy was represented in the theatre of that city, in the year 1812.

A report was circulated that the play, notwithstanding its title, and the ancient persons evoked upon the scene, was an allegorical composition: Ajax was General Moreau; Agamemnon, Bonaparte. The fears of the police were excited, and a prohibition was sent to the actors, prohibiting them from performing that play. Not contented with the success of this perfidy, the writers sold to the officers of police six articles from their journal to prove, not that Ajax was a poor play, but that Foscolo, from his political opinions, deserved the rigour of government. A trifling circumstance, of which the annals of the stage offers more than one example, increased the dismay of the author of *Ajax;* the word *Salamani,* which is the Italian for the inhabitants of *Salamis,* has another more popular acceptation; it is the diminutive of *salame,* sausages. Ajax, who, in the tragedy, frequently addresses his dear *Salaminiens,* was obliged to repeat the word with such ludicrous associations; imagine the buffoonery of a hero, before an audience disposed to lay hold of the pun, exclaiming: " *O carissimi Salamini !*" or, " *O dear little sausages !*" The new tragedy of the young man was, besides, very wearisome. The disloyal arms which his enemies employed caused in Foscolo the keenest irritation. They replied to his fury by epigrams. The best was from Monti.

" For twenty-two years," said Foscolo to me, " I was the giant of the fable ; encompassed by enemies, disappointed in my political hopes, harassed as a poet, and banished from my native city, I passed my time in avenging myself."

Foscolo wrote a book in the Vulgate Latin, immolating all his enemies in a holocaust. The book has nerve and wit, but it is too bitter for buffoonery, and too caustic for gaiety. Besides darting his poisoned arrows at his enemies, he plants his heavy artillery against his country, which he thought deserving of a heavy bombardment. He called his satire an imitation of Sterne's "*Sentimental Journey*," but it is no more like the original pleasantry and quaint melancholy humour of Sterne, than the vehement *Letters of Ortis* are like the solemn musings of Werter. The admirable poem of *Des Tombeaux*, succeeded this anathema. Europe recognizes it as one of the master-pieces of modern literature. He also pronounced an excellent discourse at Milan upon the " *Origin and Duties of Literature*," which gained him a nomination, after Monti, for Professor of Literature in the University of Pavia.

The Austrians, when seizing Italy, banished Foscolo for life. He passed to Switzerland, from thence to England.

Foscolo's literary character was formed from a mixture of different elements ; the misanthropy of Rousseau, was expressed in the turgid style of Seneca. He was an admirer of classic forms, and was imbued also with a love for the melancholy and depth of English tragedy ; he endeavoured to accomplish a fusion between these two tendencies ; an idea not without its grandeur, but in which the defect of primitive unity was evident. Whatever was strong was sure of his suffrage ; he admired the majesty of the Hebrew poetry ;

the pompous energy of Lucan ; also the rude and bold sententiousness of Alfieri. He confounded the various sources of the sublime in these writers, and did not perceive that they were incongruous and could not unite. The Italian Ortis expressed the sorrows of Werter in the turgid style of Seneca ; the Homeric Ajax gives vent and grief to his despair with Hamlet's wild fancies and fitful gleams. Alfieri, in subjecting modern subjects to the severe and stately form of Grecian tragedy, fell into the same error. When I became an inmate with this other Alfieri, lyrical and erudite ; when I witnessed his furious misanthropy and classical pedantry, though united with strength and spirit ; when I heard him rave against destiny ; when I saw him in dishabille, with his affections and childish egotism, I felt how much was factitious and how little vital in that species of literature and genius. No root unites it to the present living world ; to the real passions of men, to the interests and ideas of the future ; but with so much that was artificial, he did indeed possess real talent, brilliant eloquence, an enthusiastic love of liberty and hatred of oppression, which interested me deeply.

Foscolo's literary taste improved and his power augmented after he came to England ; among a practical people, his literary productions were less vehement and declamatory ; but his disposition altered not ; he created as many enemies in London as in Venice. He published some works in England ; his hymns to Canova, and poem entitled the Graces, are of admirable purity ; he also wrote many excellent articles in the Quarterly and Edinburgh Reviews.

It was at the time of his great literary success, when he was patronized by the most distinguished men in England, that I was introduced to him. His vehement manner produced upon me the effect of theatrical declamation ; patriotism, as represented by him, wore a Grecian mask, and was mounted upon the stilts of the Hellenic Medea and Clytemnestra. This paganism revived ill-suited my taste ; I felt the artifice.

When Foscolo described to me, true Venetian as he was, the tedium of London and the numerous misadventures that had welcomed him in this land of Cyclops, as he called England, he was infinitely more entertaining ; he returned to nature.

"*Sono Bestia*," said he to me, whilst walking the room, "these English are brutes. Doubly Teutonic, these Cyclops cannot comprehend poetry ! Ah ! I bitterly lament my youth, my quarrels at the theatre, the sun of Venice ; my heroic posture in Ajax anathematized. I live a life in this English isle, hemmed in on every side like the stabled ox ; it weighs me down. They *dare* to patronize me ! I am their pet and idol. I scorn them ! and I wish them to know it."

He died insolvent, and the Cyclops paid his funeral expenses.

CHAPTER III.

A VISIT TO BENTHAM.

I WENT with my friend Brown to visit that La Fontaine among philosophers, Jeremy Bentham, who was, like his prototype, a true child in the simplicity of his tastes, and in his social life.   We found him in a house overlooking West-minster Park, in which house he had passed the last thirty years of his anchorite life ; be rarely went out, and saw but little of the world.   The philosopher met us, dressed with philosophic negligence : the collar of his shirt falling over, his frock-coat, with only one row of buttons, merely for the necessity of closing it ; his half-boots, of antique style, and above them mixed hose ; here was the strange accoutrement which participated at once of the simplicity of the college and the ancient garb still worn by some of the contemporaries of George III.

It is impossible to imagine a greater contrast than that which existed between the classical radical, Homeric and vehement, and the English utilitarian radical ; so calm and gentle in demeanour.   The vociferous Foscolo founded no school.   The peaceable Bentham reduced to a rationale for the use of England the theories of the eighteenth century, and never did peaceable philosopher dwelling in abstractions take captive the spirits of men to such an extent. An entire party accepted him for their oracle.

At the commencement of the nineteenth century Jeremy Bentham was in the acme of his glory. At the dawn of this rising luminary, the Empress Catherine of Russia received his letters and replied to them. The Emperor Alexander, when in London, visited him, and the philosopher had the noble pride of presenting to the autocrat a gilded snuff-box, a gift from the Empress, and adorned with her miniature.

Between 1820 and 1825, Bentham was but little esteemed by the English, although celebrated throughout Europe, and enjoying from that time an immense popularity in the New World. In 1820 Hobhouse and Rolls were more popular than he in the parks and squares of London. At New York and in Calcutta, Bentham carried the day beyond all contemporary celebrities. The small number of visitors he received were admitted one after another, as in a confessional ; chief of a sect, he loved not to talk before witnesses ; and though a great talker, he occupied himself only with facts.

After welcoming my friend and myself, he proposed to us to take some turns with him in his garden ; a utilitarian recreation by which he could exercise for his health whilst conversing with friends, and indoctrinating them. The old man, whilst pacing the alleys, his spirit effervescing with a thousand thoughts, dilated with warmth upon the plans he meditated, and the bright future which awaited the people.

I was touched by his evident sincerity, and dissatisfied with his doctrines, which were daughters of calculation and materialism.   Whilst he was talking with me, too, I felt that he would repose the same confidence in the first transatlantic adventurer or charlatan whom he should meet, and that he would expound to them, as to me, a constitution for the first desert isle which should fall in his way.   During this time he ran, rather than walked.   His voice was clear, but piercing, and his sentences frequently broken.   He regarded neither elegance of manner, costume, or motion.   He at length halted before two magnificent cotton trees, at the extremity of the garden, and, inscribed upon the wall, overshadowed by their summits, he read to me these words : *"Dedicated to the Prince of Poets."*   In effect, it was in a house situated upon this spot where the great Milton long lived.   "My young friend," said he, " I intend to cut down these trees, and transform the residence of Milton, the cradle of *Paradise Lost*, into a *Chrestomatic School!*   Are you still a prey to the poetical illusions of which the world boasts ?   So much the worse for you !"

" Thus," thought I, " in this hallowed spot, where the great poet respired heaven's free air, enjoying in solitude his genius with her celestial visions, will daily assemble a boisterous multitude, desecrating this sacred ground by their profane wrangling !"

Bentham divined my thought, and replied to it, saying : " I do not contemn Milton, but he belongs to the past, and is of no use to this age."

After all, Milton, who was the chief of a school, was not without resemblance to Bentham; there was the same puritanical gravity of expression, united with gentleness, the same excitability of temperament, corrected by habit and reason; the voices would have chimed, being clear and sonorous, and the hair of both flowed negligently. I thought, also, I perceived some resemblance between the philosopher and Franklin and Fox, though the countenance of the former was more expressive of sport and humour; Bentham's eye had the restless and ardent gaze upon vacancy as had Fox's; but Bentham's seemed in quest of invisible algebraic problems, and descrying in the distance circles and parallelograms.

Notwithstanding his gentleness, I was ill at ease with this schoolman and materialist. What sympathy could enter his heart for me? None. He was in abstract regions, submitting the facts he had collected to a dialectic process, and arranging them into a subtle system; that was his pleasure. There was nothing haughty, arbitrary, or misanthropical in his looks or deportment; the good-humoured man thought not of himself, nevertheless he thought no more of me; he would have given thirty thousand men for one axiom, the whole human race for a theory.

"I would wish," said he to me, "that each remaining year of my life could be separated from the natural succession, and that after my death I could enjoy one year at the end of so many centuries; I should then witness the influence that my works had exercised."

Alas! will they live so long? Has Bentham really given

a new impulse to humanity ? No. Algebraist in social science, he allows nothing for the varieties and inconsistencies of human nature. "Who, in steering his course," said the poet, "heeds not the caprices of the wind, is not a skilful pilot." Bentham, the rigid calculator, treated of man as a reasonable and logical animal, not as an imperfect, passionate, and impulsive being. O, moralist ! you forget that we are composed of sympathies and antipathies ; that is to say, we are infirm in our nature, and man is not God.

In this consists the error of the nineteenth century,—the deification of man,—the apotheosis of reason. In hearkening to Bentham, I again met the theories in which my youth had been nurtured ; I distrusted this modern and singular sophism. In doing good we feel pleasure, therefore pleasure is goodness, and goodness is pleasure ;—certainly will has its pleasure ; is not then vice and pleasure the same thing ? What folly ! to confound what should be the result of goodness with the motive; and to identify animal pleasure with religion and pure happiness.

These thoughts were passing confusedly through my mind, when a few drops of rain warned us to return to the house. The philosopher seated himself at his piano and began to play ; but first fixed his eyes upon a verdant lawn in order to refresh his spirits, as he told us, for a work upon the reform of prisons. He was then engaged in planning a circular panopticon, a sort of transparent hive, where each of the morally diseased could dwell apart ; he was to be placed in the middle, and from that central point take note of the acts of each individual ; to preach to his brother man, give him work, remove every temptation to sin ; feed, warm, and clothe him ; then, after having convinced him, partly by force, partly by arguments, that all was for his good, he hoped to open the portals and return the brotherhood to society perfectly sound.

"O philosopher !" said I, in quitting him, " you know less upon this point than the mere vagrant in the corner of the streets ; you are ignorant of the seductions and wild enterprise of the erratic and vagrant life.   O innocent and gentle philosopher ! you know not what it is to brave peril, feel life keenly, enjoy a ferocious independence."

The Utopian, in taking leave of me, presented me with an enormous packet of his works, which I still own ; they are in my library side by side with the works of Fourier.   Notwithstanding my veneration for the gentle philosopher, I departed with a feeling of sadness for his monomania. Brown told me he had only a bare support ; his eccentricities in taste, and his love of novel and bold speculations, had dissipated his patrimony.   The projectors of plans for the amelioration and progress of the human race ruin him ; as soon as their reasoning appears to him solid, his fortune is at their service. He is brother-in-law to Abbott, formerly speaker in the House of Commons, now Lord Colchester.   When a member of Eton College, poetry was his abomination, but prosody was his pleasure ; that was a numerical science.   He loved, as a scholar, to scan the verses of Virgil ; or, like a professor, to discuss the employ of the

Grecian participles.   Amateur of the engravings from Hogarth, he appreciated the analytical sublimity of that artist. One of his *useful* recreations, which he succeeds in very well, is turning ; he has many little instruments and articles of furniture which display his skill in that art.

"I understand," replied I to Brown ; " and he takes men for clumps or wooden blocks that he can fashion, turn, and polish."

CHAPTER IV.

IMPROVISATIONS OF COLERIDGE.

THE good Elizabeth was not pleased to hear that I had had an interview with Bentham ; then there was more odium than celebrity attached to his name, and all thorough Calvinists viewed him as an insidious and dangerous innovator.   Elizabeth, author of many works upon the education of children, was gentle and mild in the domestic circle, inflexible in doctrines, lovely and benignant in disposition; but severe in her religious requirements, she offered a singular type of an austere and visionary, though worldly fanatic.   I had seen nothing similar in my country.

It was natural that she should not approve of my visit to Jeremy Bentham ; so, as a counterbalance to what she styled my fault, she insisted that I should be introduced to the truly great men, the religious men of her country ; and first and foremost in the ranks stood Samuel Taylor Coleridge, who dwelt near London, in a modest retreat, where his friends would assemble and listen to his eloquence.   Deistical philosopher in his youth, and one of the chiefs of the poetical reform, he had become a Christian mystic.   He

alone in England occupied a place analagous with that of
Schelling, Fichte, and Hegel ; but the eminently practical
spirit of England tendered him more admiration than disciples.

We arrived at eight at the small but elegant residence of
Coleridge ; about thirty persons were already assembled in
a small blue room, simply furnished. Coleridge was dis-
coursing. Standing in front of the chimney upon which he
leaned back, with head erect and arms crossed, his dreamy
eyes lost in abstractions, transported by the inspirations of
his own genius, he seemed to be addressing, not the auditors,
but replying to his own thoughts. His voice was vibratory,
rich and full, his features harmonious, his ample brow,
shaded by dark brown curls, in which here and there some
silver lines intruded, the beautiful contour of his mouth,
sweet in expression, also the softness of his expressive eyes,
won favour unheard. He recalled to my mind the physiognomy of Fox, with more of calm ; that of Mirabeau, with
less turbulence ; and that of M. Berryer, with a disposition
more abstract and dreamy. Like these three remarkable
men he was endowed with the first gift for the orator, sym-
pathetic force. Surrounded by a circle who enkindled the
enthusiasm which was transmitted in full power in return,
he went on with an erudite and masterly analysis of the
dramatic poets of Greece. It is only in the personal presence of the great Sorcerer that his ideas upon these sublime
dramatists can be imparted ; in his own nervous style he
described the subtle reasoning and the pathos of Euripides,

the harmonious and celestial grace that characterized Sopho-
cles, and the lofty but solemn eloquence of Eschylus. During ten minutes, he commented upon the Prometheus of
Eschylus, the ode to Destiny, and the pleading of man
against Providence. By degrees, as the orator raised the
triple veil which enwraps the allegory, his eye gleams, his
animation becomes vehemence, and by his anguish and
energy he reproduces before our eyes the victim of destiny,
marked for the vengeance of the Gods. We see him pouring
out his plaints and laments to the winds which war around
his devoted head,—sublime emblem of the ancient and terrible belief in fatality. Soon the mythological type gives
place to the destiny of the Christian man, and in the most
bold and brilliant style he follows, and elucidates all the
metaphysical theories upon the enigma of life. He traces
Hartley through the labyrinth of his aerial tissues, weighs
the mystic chain of associations, explains the chimeras of
the will, brings all the weight of argument to the metaphysical contest between the spiritualists and materialists, and
treads with a heavy foot the enchanted domain of Berkley.[*]

He cited the strong eloquence of Tillotson and Clark, and
reaching Leibnitz, he followed that great philosopher over
the bridge of communication which he extended from earth
to heaven. Leibnitz led to Spinoza. We heard him with
the ardent glow of genius refute the impalpable pantheism of

---

[*] There are several other names and theories introduced by Coleridge
as subjects of discourse, but not of much present interest.

Spinoza, who gave a soul to the universe without individuality, and motion to matter without a mover. In the mazes of these metaphysical speculations, the poetic genius of Coleridge would flow on, or disport in circles like the harmonious and luminous ocean. From the refutation of Spinoza, " who," says he, " withdraws God from the universe," he proceeded in beautiful and sublime strains to illustrate the tenets and principles of religion, till, reached to the summit, where he could advance no farther or higher, he bowed himself in humility and reverence to the earth, and murmuring some sweet and mysterious verses from Dante's Paradise, he closed.

I withdrew, filled with the highest and deepest admiration. Never had I seen in human being the union of such glowing eloquence and subtle acumen.

Three days after this, by my own request I was introduced to him; and in many conversations, which might rather be called monologues and dithyrambic strains, he condescended to reveal to me the principal points of his great system. He repudiated none of the dogmas of Christianity, for he believed they were conformable with reason, experience, and history. The material mystery of life, or the physical union which produced the phenomena, he thought was electricity, magnetism, and galvanism, which seemed to him to accord with the spiritual mystery of the soul associated to an intelligence served by organs. He thought all philosophical doctrines were explained through Christianity, which contained them all. He believed in progress developing itself through the phases of humanity; and in traditions of the past, vege-

6

tation becoming animal life in its progress, and the lower animal ascending to the higher. In all his conversations which were not direct instruction, one could not but lament some obscurity and mistiness; but in listening and endeavouring to follow him, I experienced nothing of that weariness and disgust that the systems of Bentham caused in me, neither that vacuum which the theatrical and pompous Foscolo induced. Vibrating to all emotions, capable of comprehending all systems, possessing rich treasures of memory and a truly independent spirit, with a taste for all philosophical reveries and caprices, and luxuriating in beauty, with the ability to reproduce his brilliant and deep thought with all the fascinations of genius, Coleridge appeared to me a sort of mystical Diderot. Unhappily, the feebleness of his frame, much increased from his fatal indulgence in opium, did not permit him to draw up as a whole his magnificent system of æsthetic Christianity, of which he has only bequeathed some vestiges.

It would be impossible to enumerate the variety and depth of studies from which he reaped such fruits. He was familiar with the brilliant prose of Jeremy Taylor, the sonnets of Bowles, and the essays of Addison; also the works of Jean Jacques and Rabelais, Crébillon and Goldsmith, enchanted him. Romance, history, poetry, the dramatic art, the fine arts, he essayed them all, and enjoyed all. The erudite and occult sciences claimed his regard; the metaphysics of Fichte, Kant, Winckelman, and Hegel counted him among their adepts. Coleridge has neared all shores. When the popular fury crushed the towers of the Bastile, his muse rang the peal of joy; poet, philosopher, artist, critic, man of taste and erudition, he has dispensed but scattered rays of light. The fault is not alone his, but that of his age and country.

The practical world around cannot comprehend him. The renown of the utilitarian Bentham augmented each day, whilst that of the mystical Coleridge was contested or decried. But time, the great restorer, has set all right. The fragments of Coleridge, his prose so philosophic and brilliant, his inspired poetry, in fine, his admirable autobiography, in which he shows himself devoid of the egotistical spirit, but psychologically profound, assign him a niche unique among philosophers and poets of the nineteenth century. He was the Novalis of England.

A Visit to South Stack.

IN 1822 I became acquainted with a brave sea captain, named Patrick O'Mealy, from Ireland, as his name indicates. I first met with him at the house of the ingenious Porden, architect of George III., and guilty of having built the Chinese Pavilions with little steeples in Brighton, which makes the little city a finished model of bad taste. O'Mealy, like all the Irish, doated upon his country. "The Saxon Isle," he said to me, is nothing; "all there is flat and tame, of no beauty. A stranger who has not seen Ireland is unacquainted with England. Only devote two months to Ireland, and, my word for it, you will see something. We will start on Monday, steer straight to Anglesea, where I have a small house; from there you can go to Dublin when you choose."

There is a freshness of feeling in youth, and a power of unhackneyed observation, which gives a peculiar charm to early travels. I joined O'Mealy, and sailed for Ireland. Our intention was to visit South Stack. There is no place less known, more rarely visited, or more curious. As these seas are dangerous, and the material interests of life do not call strangers to this coast, you scarcely meet a person. It was necessary to traverse the extent of the English isle, from the county of Middlesex to Bangor in Caernarvon; to quit London, the lap of luxury, for strange and isolated regions, protected by a chain of rocks from the invasion of British ideas and customs. We paused on our route to view Oxford and her colleges, Birmingham with her industrial activity, Worcester, rich in historical recollections. As soon as we entered the country of Wales, we found the names as unpronounceable (for instance, Alamvruft, Drwsquantucha) as their acclivities were inaccessible. At the extreme point of this country, on the Irish side, is the island of Auglesea, or *Anglo-Sea*. A little islet of rocks detached from this angle is called South Stack by the peasants, *Holyhead* upon the maps. This islet is opposite to the Bay of Dublin, and is separated from it by the narrowest part of the Irish Channel. Nothing can be more tumultuous than the sea in this passage. Rocks and ocean seem to place a barrier between the two inimical countries of England and Ireland. Conceive of ships passing through two jagged coasts, overhung with cliffs and crags, the furious waves lashing their sides as they rush foaming through the crevices of the rocks; add to this the whirlpools ready to engulph the ship as she reels and staggers, now this way, now that, the sport of winds and waves; fortunate if she escape being locked in, as with grappling irons, between two contiguous rocks in her narrow course.* In the ship's career,

---

* Such has been the fate of a vessel; it mounted aloft between two rocks, but was freed by the skill of the captain.

as she is lifted or cast down by a wave, you see at a distance to the west a revolving light, now red, then pale, scintillating, purple or wan by turns, her uncertain rays illumining the horizon. When the ship mounts the star is eclipsed, when she sinks, and her sails are under water, it reappears. In the surrounding darkness it is a picturesque spectacle, a planet so changeable yet so constant in her evolution. This light indicates to you South Stack. Traversing the same seas by day, you perceive a white tower suspended from a crag; the ship proceeds; then you discover a little islet near by Holyhead, which serves as a base for this turret; then, as you approach, you see a species of wire net-work suspended, which serves as a point of communication between the little isle with the tower and the torn summits of the rock opposite. Upon this net-work, which at a distance looks as fragile as the spider's web, you see human beings passing and repassing in mid-air. An active circulation is established upon this hanging bridge. Man, a moving atom, how small he appears! You see around you the ocean, the heavens, and the rocks, and you take pity upon the masters of the world, who appear to you from these summits like pucerons on the pistil of a flower. The excessive tenuity of this bridge suspended in the air, and which appears still lighter when compared with gigantic nature around, makes it seem as a fairy tissue, upheld by fairy power.

Captain O'Mealy was right. Nature and art have combined and issued their fiat that the South Stack is worthy of commemoration.

I have passed with O'Mealy many delightful hours upon the rocks and strands of this singular shore, and I dub myself as historiographer in fee simple of this unrecorded domain. My chronicle speaks not of kings dethroned or battles gained, but of conquests obtained over nature's bulwarks, of peculiarities before unremarked; and the heroes are the inhabitants of the air and the waters. "The lighthouse, whose picturesque aspect we have admired," said O'Mealy, "owed its birth to the perils of these shores. At some seasons the currents and counter-currents in these seas meet in a vortex; then woe to the poor mariners who are drawn within the circle; the firmest and most experienced navigators, the strongest and best-manned ships, cannot escape the yawning gulf. A few years since, the people upon the heights around saw a brig disappear, masts, cordage, rigging, crew, without resistance, or possibility of averting the catastrophe; they were in a moment ingulphed in the vortex. We frequently, during the long winter nights, hear the signal of distress; in the morning, some scattered wrecks proclaim that this Charybdis hath swallowed a new prey."

Arrived at Anglesea, we reposed some days at the house of O'Mealy; then, seizing a favourable day and wind, we embarked in a little yacht which belonged to the captain, and was steered by an experienced Irish pilot, who from his youth had been accustomed to steering along these shores.

It was a beautiful morning in the beginning of June; a light breeze wafted us from the east, and the sea was calm. However, with all our precautions, we were sometimes in peril, both from the reefs and also sand-banks : here were some reefs level with the water, which the natives call *platters*, and more than one keel of a vessel has been destroyed by these unseen enemies lurking in the deep; the sand-banks are not less dangerous.   Upon our route we remarked the triumphant arch built of black Anglesea marble, to commemorate the visit of George IV. to the Isle of Mona.

We passed in our yacht some remarkable forms among the rocks.   The hand of the architect could not have formed better colonnades, pillars, arches, and cornices.   There never was an aspect of nature more wild, and at the same time more beautiful.   Beneath these overhanging rocks which menace us are caves, the entrances to which are lined with figures that seem exquisitely moulded in all the forms of statuary and architecture.   When the waters are low you can enter without difficulty within the largest of these subterranean palaces.   Nothing can exceed the beauty of the portal of this cave as you see it from your yacht.   The opening is round, as if by measurement of the most perfect geometrician ; this circle serves as a frame for marine mosses which trellis it.   At the risk of slipping over the marine algas, or sinking in the dashing waves which in their retreat would roll back upon us, we entered nature's portal, and passing through fragments of rocks, which seemed, as in a freak of nature, to assume every form of Gothic and arabesque figure, we reached what the people around call the *chamber of parliament.*   There you seat yourself amid a population as prating and bustling as is the crowd of our

orators and politicians.   Here commences the empire of the
birds.   When a stranger appears among them, discord and
dismay fill the realm.   You see them flutter, you hear their
wails, for five minutes the air is darkened, the ear is stunned
with the flapping of their wings and the noise of their flight.
All that lives and moves along these caves and grottoes is
the winged race.   From every crevice, gap, and dark winding passage issue such swarms of sea-birds, that they fall in
heaps before your eyes, their white breasts and black wings,
with soft glow-worm lustre peering through the darkness.
This region is exclusively the bird region ; birds nestle upon
the rocks, they walk upon the waves, the sand-banks and
shores.   Nothing is more singular than the complete line of
demarcation which separates the different tribes of the
winged race ; they hold themselves invariably within certain
limits which they never pass over, excepting the gulls, whose
nature is more volatile, and they circulate with freedom and
independence among various tribes.

In the centre of this amphitheatre of rocks, mostly of
jagged and grotesque forms, you see one of enormous surface, recently rent by the thunder.   There is a singular
avenue opened in this rock from the recession of the massive
parts.   This phenomenon is not uncommon.   In the beds of
gigantic rocks, you see longitudinal fissures, the work of
nature and time, but which appear the beautiful effect of
design.   Religious traditions have consecrated this passage
or gap just mentioned.   A pure serpentine stream courses
within, which is renowned for its healing virtues, and held in
6*

great veneration in the country. It is not fifty years since there was to be seen upon the summit of the rock a little chapel, which is now ruined, the Delphos temple of this mysterious fountain.

There was a singular fête celebrated at this fountain once a year ; the first three Sundays in July were consecrated to it. The young lads and lasses of the neighbourhood descended together to the spring ; there each one, after filling both hands with sand and the mouth with water, was to ascend the narrow sloping path without spilling a grain of sand or losing a drop of water ; the happy youth or maiden who had succeeded in this enterprise was sure to marry within the year the object of love. In 1770, there was a morose priest who guarded the flock in these regions, whom this ingenious custom filled with horror. He saw in it the remnants of damnable idolatry; and not content to thunder from the pulpit against the paganism of his flock, he destroyed from the foundations the chapel of Lockwood, choked up the avenue, and filled the bed of the stream with gravel and stones. Now all that remains of this rustic chapel is only a few fragments on the top of the rock, which is in keeping with the wild scenery around. In effect, these blocks of rough granite, mingled with the wrecks of Gothic sculpture in this wild place, seems like a ruin.

You should not approach South Stack, or rather the amphitheatre of rocks which have that name, in full day ; the lines are not definite ; you lose the characteristics of the scenery ; but if you enter the bay at sunrise, every outline will be definitely marked, the hanging bridge suspended from one rock to another, the bend of the bay, and the whimsical forms the rocks and crags assume in the lights and shadows, the mysterious fount of which you trace the course by the discoloured rock, and, to complete the scene, the light of aurora shows up another cavern, by which our yacht anchored amid the roaring waves. A large flight of steps cut in the rock led us to the most elevated part of the islet; before us was the suspended bridge. We had a commanding view of the whole maritime prospect; but the chronicles of South Stack contain a series of shipwrecks, and to this she owes her ingenious lighthouse, which has given her celebrity.

Various are the sad annals of shipwrecks upon this rock-bound coast. One cold winter's night, in 1808, during a tempestuous snow-storm, a ship was wrecked against a shelving rock, and the crew were found the next morning in situations which showed that the poor creatures had struggled hard to escape death, and many were frozen in the attempt. The captain seemed to have resigned himself with fortitude to inevitable destiny; his head reposed upon his uplifted hands, he was sheltered under a projecting rock, and seemed to have fallen asleep in that posture. The sailors were dispersed at different distances, according as their strength permitted them to escape, at a farther or shorter distance from the raging billows; death had surprised them in the midst of a painful struggle to avoid it. One sailor was frozen in the act of climbing a rock; another whilst wiping his brow, which was covered with snow; a third, exhausted with his efforts, was seating himself. One of these poor wretches had obtained a secure shelter, when the current of his blood froze in his veins.

Frequently, during a fog, ships which had deviated some knots or fathoms were swallowed in the vortex in a moment. In 1826, a fine brig, newly built, named *Alexander*, in a thick fog was drawn towards the vortex, when her keel struck against the reefs. There the poor ship vacillated as upon a pivot, beating her flanks and her rigging, as a flail thrashes the grain : imagine the situation of the passengers at this crisis. The master carpenter proposed to them a means of escape. The bowsprit nearly touched the point of a rock, and from that crag one might reach a neighbouring plateau, but not without danger. Back of this plateau was an inaccessible wall of hard and polished stone. A young Englishman from Kingston hazarded the first leap. Two ladies, three children, an English and a Spanish merchant followed, and soon the whole crew reached this plateau, where they were entirely cut off from the world, without power to make themselves heard or obtain any relief. The night was cold and dark, the rain fell, the passengers and sailors were pressed together in a small space, which scarcely sufficed for them to stand upon ; the least movement would have precipitated into the flood many of these poor creatures, who were constrained under penalty of death to remain fixed in the same posture they had first taken.

The flood threatened to overtake them. They saw the ocean billows mounting towards them, roaring, swelling, sweeping along the base of the little plain upon which they stood, and rushing on to devour them. How shun this death when they could measure its progress, and calculate its proximity, which was momentarily increasing. The wall behind them appeared inaccessible, and the tide still arose. There was only a foot and a half between them and the sea, when the tide stood still, then began to recede. At length day dawned; a young cabin-boy climbed upon the shoulders of one of his comrades, and then climbed up the bulwark, and when he reached the summit, he drew, by means of re-iterated signals, the attention of some of the inhabitants of the coast, who threw up cords, and ropes fastened to the rock secured their safety. One alone among them, whose leg struck violently against a rock, fell into the sea, and there perished.

Captain Evans, master of the harbour of Holyhead, was the first to suggest to the government the idea of construct-ing a lighthouse upon this island, which was with such dif-ficulty visited on account of the dangerous rocks. The numerous accidents rendered such a precaution indispensable. The work was commenced in 1808: a temporary shelter was constructed for the workmen, and the superintendence of the labour was confided to the captain. The communication be-tween the island and the coast was then much more difficult than at this day: people could only land upon the island on the south-east side, and then they must consult the tide, and mount with the waves. How could they in such a situation maintain seventy workmen, and not only supply them with food, but also with materials for building and tools to work with, upon an island whose barriers were rocks, and whose Cerberus a whirlpool, and whose only port threatened enormous dangers ?   A plan was devised and adopted of attaching a ferry-boat, by means of very strong cables and pullies, to one of the crags on the coast, and one on the island, and by this means draw up the materials for the workmen.   It was expressly prohibited that the workmen should absent themselves more than one day in the week, and that should be Sunday, if the weather was not tempestuous.   One young mason, exiled in the solitary isle, received tidings in the middle of the week of the dangerous illness of his mother. The superintendent of the work was absent; the sea was turbulent, and the young man in passionate grief at the idea of his mother's agony.   After having vainly endeavoured to procure a boat, he took this bold resolution: he secured himself by cables in the ferry-boat, and was borne in the machine through the air to the rocks of the opposite shore.   The astonished and terrified spectators followed him with their eyes during his aërial voyage.   When the superintendent returned, he prohibited under severe penalties that such a dangerous experiment should ever be renewed; but on the young mason, whose filial piety had braved death, there was no chastisement imposed.

After this there was an addition contrived in the ferry-boat for the accommodation of travellers through the air; a species of moveable cradle was attached to the boat—a whimsical affair which for a long time was used, transported people bold enough to adventure themselves, or who were forced to make a virtue of necessity. Scarcely a deer would have confided itself without fear even to the difficult foot-path which led to the point of embarcation, and afterwards for a route of one hundred and fifty feet balanced in the air and supported by a cable above the foaming sea. It was necessary to arm one's self with presence of mind and courage. Captain Evans first tested this singular car. Sometimes three or four workmen would seat themselves there together, and tossed by the sea-breeze, would gaily accomplish their voyage between sky and water. Three English ladies attempted this inconvenient mode of transportation; the sea became high and the breeze strong, so that half way in her course the men could not impel the machine: the voyagers remained there an hour, cradled in the storm, enjoying at leisure the sublime perspective, listening to the roaring of the floods—an admirable situation for meditating philosophically upon the causes of the picturesque and upon the beauties of nature. Add to this view the whirlpool ready to embrace them, the creaking and whizzing of their air carriage, and the roar of distant thunder.

By degrees these difficulties were overcome, and terrors abated. Convenient steps were hollowed from the rock; a simple bridge from crag to crag has taken the place of the cradle, a balustrade, or rather a double wall, protects feeble heads against vertigo. In the mean time, the vibrations and trembling of the wooden bridge extended over cables could not allay the fears of those whose nerves were sensitive.

Five years after, the wire bridge (which stands at this day) was constructed upon the principle of perfect solidity and rare elegance: a troop of horsemen might venture to cross it.

In the mean time the work went on; the Pharos was built, and lighted mariners in February, 1809. It is of simple style, solid, and the walls at their base are five feet in thickness. The lantern is two hundred feet above the level of the water. There are three reflectors, and the spring of a clock connected with the mirrors gives them a rotatory movement. They revolve in two minutes, which produces a very picturesque effect, as a light constantly changing, but ever fixed in its evolutions. The design of this peculiar mechanism is, that it may not be confounded with the light from the Skerry Isles. The light from South Stack is perceived at nine leagues' distance in the most stormy weather.

One time the sea penetrated through these walls of five feet thickness; the fury of the waves destroyed some of the masonry, and caused a gap; also the interior walls of the edifice were constantly damp, and the foundations of the lighthouse itself were undermined. The architect endeavoured to strengthen and secure the base with large bands of copper, then he added new layers of cement to the old. All known means were employed without success, and many new plans were devised. The mixture of iron filings with ashes and lime to fill the interstices and crevices was tried; but even this solid substance could not resist the continued action of the waves. The water still rushed through. At length an old ship painter, whom Captain Evans knew, communicated to him a fact opportunely to save the lighthouse of South Stack from imminent peril. A ruin was discovered buried in the earth and decayed, excepting a part painted with oil paint, mixed with fine sand and lead. There was a chemical analysis, and the ingredients of the paint were ascertained. The experiment was tried with the lighthouse; it was painted with two coats of this paint, and from that time no water has penetrated through the wall, or injured the edifice.

Thus a wild and sterile island, which was rented for a pound sterling a year, and scarcely could feed two sheep, has become an object worthy of interest. Numerous travellers expose themselves to the dangers of the sea to visit it, fearing no longer the Charybdis of these shores.

There are evident marks in the island, and the region around, of some violent convulsion of nature. The geologist, in a visit to South Stack, will find much to interest. The ornithologist and naturalist might remain there a long time with profit and pleasure. No where do our winged friends enjoy more complete liberty. I seated myself upon a projecting rock for two hours, observing their flights, and listening to their intonations as they mingled their lugubrious cries with the roar of the ocean. From every chink, gap, and cranny, issue birds; every rock is colonized by birds, but more especially the caverns are their domain. O'Mealy had spoken to me of this cavern, and I determined to visit it; he accompanied me, and we breakfasted gaily there upon some cuts of smoked ham. Now I could truly say that I had lived with the birds.

We counted in a lateral niche sixty dozen of the sea turtle-dove, and we seated ourselves so as not to lose any of their movements. This race of birds is heavy and ordinary in their exterior. Near them, but without mixing, were the penguins, the dandies of this solitude. When I drew near they paid no attention to me, but they were distant in their manners, and would not be greeted. I admired the familiarity of the sea-mew, especially a small species ; this bird flapped against my hair with his wing, then he would fly some feet distant, pouring out his sweet and plaintive notes, and look at me with an air of the most simple surprise.

Without the cave I saw some isolated eggs upon the smooth acclivity of a rock. " By what instinct or miracle," said I to Captain O'Mealy, " do these eggs hold themselves there ?" He explained the phenomena by saying that a viscous matter attached them to the rock. In fact, once move them, and you cannot place them there again.

Though so numerous at this day, before the construction of the Pharos I was told that the birds were ten times more numerous. The sound of the hammer and the rending of rocks offended the bird population, and they flew off *en masse ;* the emigration was general. Two solitary gulls, in the mean time, had courage to brave the invaders, and they posted themselves upon the peak of a naked rock, where a stone or a gun could easily dislodge them. This confidence was recompensed, however, for orders were given not to molest them. The old birds, familiarizing themselves to the noise of the workmen, profited by the permission granted

them, and for five successive years had returned to occupy
their old nest. This lesson was not lost upon the race of
gulls. After their emigration, finding themselves disturbed
by the children who hunted for eggs in the holes in the rocks,
they returned to the islands and to their ancient asylums.
The orders for their protection and security were renewed,
the use of firearms was prohibited, and soon the plain was
covered with nests. Now, it would be impossible to cross
this space after the eggs are deposited without destroying a
multitude of them. The sea turtle-doves and penguins have
returned also, but in less numbers.

During half the year, the gulls absent themselves from
South Stack ; the night of the 10th of February witnesses
their return, which is announced with great clamour ; you
would say that in returning again to the scenes of their loves
and the home of their young ones, they could not contain
their joy. During eight days they flutter around, rather
than assemble in a body ; it is a democratic tumult ; afterwards they organize the republic, then each couple separate
themselves, and begin to work. It is an interesting spectacle.

Few days pass in which some lads do not peril their lives
in searching for the eggs of the sea-gull, or the marine fennel
seed. This is a terrific trade, as said Shakspeare. It is
astonishing that nine-tenths of these adventurers do not
perish in the enterprise. Imagine a youth suspended by a
cord in the hands of two children younger than himself ; he
descends during a tempest or a calm, coasting a precipice,

the very sight of which makes one tremble; below him the swelling billows. As soon as he can find a narrow foothold, he halts a moment, then he crawls, climbs, slides, or drags himself until he has attained the modest treasure for which he has hazarded his life more than twenty times. Once a lady in the neighbourhood sent one of her old domestics and a child in quest of fennel; the child, suspended between the sky and the earth, had already seized the plant, when the old domestic was attacked with vertigo, being little accustomed to stand so near the abyss; she had the presence of mind to call to her aid an old woman who gathered herbs in a neighbouring field; she heard her, ran, and seized the cord just as the domestic was dropping it, and saved the child.

Some vestiges of the Romans are to be seen at South Stack; particularly some medals of Constantine, recently discovered, attest that the Romans formerly dwelt at this point of the coast. The name of Dianæ is perpetuated in these shores, as the port and isle of Diana. The sea, in laving the shore, has uncovered tombs and laid bare skeletons; some bodies were found rudely thrust into the ground, heaped pell-mell, as after a battle; others disposed with great care under plates of lead, and ornaments of all sorts were buried with them. All these bodies are laid with the head to the north.

I had passed eight days in profound solitude, when the Captain announced that we must sail for Dublin the next evening. I almost regretted having to quit the singular region which had opened scenes in nature so new to me, and so little known to the world. How could human beings exist in such a place? I had prevailed on the Captain to get a permit for us to pass a night in the lighthouse to talk with the guards; Ireland comprehends all fancies, and this of ours did not surprise the *nation*. Picture to yourself a lofty and large round column on a high arch, beat by the floods, on the top of the column a cell, and in that cell a man. I said a man: there are two; when one watches, the other sleeps. They hold conversation with the sea-mew, the waves, and the great clock of the Pharos. The watch counts the seconds by the eternal tic-tac of the pendulum whilst replenishing his lamp with oil; the lamp must be always burning. The four long months of winter pass thus; and woe to the watch if the lamp should be extinguished; there is no responsibility more weighty, and no prison life harder. The guard with whom I talked, spoke but little. He wore a strange appendage at that time—a beard as long as that of a hermit. The dialect of his native county of Cornouailles, in which he spoke, would have been hardly intelligible to me if the Captain had not translated it into English. This complete isolation has not only rendered him taciturn, but the sense of duty has reached to the degree of morbid sensibility.

" If I was to sleep whilst upon guard," said he, " and no one knew it, I should give information of myself as my brother did, whom I replace here, and who died of mortification."

I recognised here the same touching fanaticism upon the point of duty, as of the sect that became known to me in the other extremity of England, in Northumberland. The next morning we sailed for Dublin, where a people so different, so light and brilliant, would supply material for observation.

Scenes of a Life in Ireland.

A VISIT TO THE CHURCH OF ST. MICHAEL.

WHILE in Dublin, I visited the Church of St. Michael with O'Mealy, who accompanied me in all my excursions. The church is of the plainest, clumsiest, and heaviest style of Saxon architecture. The old Catholic sacristan showed us the images in his church, and recounted the various legends connected with it ; to which he added stories of the founders and repairers of the church.

The Captain listened with patience ; as for me, it was with difficulty that I could comprehend any of his Hibernian dialect, of which all the vowels were abridged, and all the hissing sounds multiplied, and uttered with a rapidity very fatiguing to the ear.

We were just quitting St. Michael's, after paying some pennies to our sacristan cicerone, when he stopped us, saying that we had not seen all ; that St. Michael's Church possessed other curiosities more interesting, and that by *Kasis !* (thus he pronounced the name of Christ) we should not leave without visiting the subterranean church, celebrated for the property of preserving uncorrupted the corpses therein laid. The guide went for his lantern, and whilst celebrating with Irish vivacity the preserving charm of this place of interment, we descended eight or ten broken steps to the oblong aisle below; the cellar was of just the dimensions of the church above.

The feeble light of the lantern scarcely dissipated the gloom around. Upon the walls and hard-trodden earthen floor there was no dampness, no odour of decomposition so revolting in approaching a mausoleum. The guide from time to time pushed aside with his foot some troublesome skull which incommoded him. " Have you seen Hamlet played ?" said O'Mealy. " Once, in Covent Garden. The beautiful Irish actress, Miss O'Neall, was Ophelia." Then O'Mealy began to repeat the lines from the English, which have become a proverb : " Did these bones cost no more the breeding than to play at loggats with them ? Mine ache to think on't." The sacristan continued to push with his foot some bones as he came across them :—" Ah ! the knave !" continued O'Mealy, " how he sports with our bones ! This might be the pate of a politician, one that would circumvent God, might it not ?"

To the right and left of this aisle, corresponding to the chapels above, were the chambers of the dead ; some were enclosed by bars, others were filled with mortal remains heaped confusedly upon one another. I saw with surprise, that time, which had spared the bodies, had not dealt thus kindly with the coffins, for the larger part had decayed.

The house of the dead was destroyed, the inhabitant was spared. Around the body we saw dust of decomposed wood, like ashes, mixed with the iron which bound the coffin. Sometimes there remained, as if to protect the body, a remnant of the coffin, as a lid, or a strip of board, along which you saw the mummy with bronzed skin.

Our guide held his lantern over those he called *his dead;* a population which submitted to his law, and upon which he levied taxes ; at the same time, he related to us, in the Irish brogue, narrations, with a queer species of buffoonery, in which you could see that the love of the sombre, common to Northern races, was mingled with brighter hues, and spiced with national humour, which is irresistibly comical. With his shrill and monotonous tones he went on repeating the old lesson ; and these mummies without name, age, or history, excepting such as are given by lying sacristans who gain their bread from exhibiting the bones, struck me with a sentiment so complex and so deep, that I was not tempted to analyze it.

The mummies were mostly black, wrinkled, and dry. The captain occasionally explained to me some of the narrations of the sacristan, who applied names and dates to these unknown remains, very much as is the custom in histories. We stood before an abbess : " Died a hundred years since," said our cicerone, " in all the odour of sanctity." She who during her life had shunned the notice of the world, was now exposed without veil to all eyes ; and she had for her neighbour an assassin, the murderer of her brother. He was an athletic man, whose long, white beard, was in complete preservation, and whose elbow touched the saint by his side. This chemical property in the crypts of St. Michael, which preserves bodies from corruption, acts in a different manner upon different constitutions and ages, and in some it has no virtue ; thus children, in whom the lymphatic element prevails, were rapidly decomposed, but old people, from the solidity of their bony system, remained perfectly sound. It appeared also that sobriety or intemperance in habits had no effect in this phenomena. The sacristan pointed out to us a celebrated drunkard and debauchee, who was a sportsman and a baronet, and died in a drunken frolic ; his flesh was in as fine preservation as that of the monk, his neighbour. Rabelais would have here found excellent reasons in favour of his divine bottle.

After having passed in review a series of corpses, black and hard, resembling each other, but in a fine state of preservation, we came to one whose arms were folded upon her breast, as if they pressed a cherished object. " This is," said our guide, " a woman who died in giving birth to an infant about fifty years since. She was placed in the coffin with the infant upon her bosom ; the child has returned to dust, but the mother is preserved." That dry and skeleton arm, still folded as if to secure the vanished treasure, was the most forcible and touching symbol of maternal love.

At the farther end of this cemetery, amongst the newest-looking coffins, we saw a sort of rude couch or boat, excavated from the trunk of an old oak, the outside still retain-

7

ing the bark.   When the lantern was directed to this spot, I noticed that the two bodies within were without heads.   I drew near, and looking attentively, I perceived that one of the two heads had been placed to the right, near the coffin; while the other, attached to the neck by one of the ligaments, had fallen over the breast of the defunct.   I walked round the coffin, and the sacristan read these words from a plate of copper nailed to one of the sides: *John and Henry Shears, Brothers*, beheaded in Dublin the 10th of April, 1799.

" Shears !" exclaimed O'Mealy; " the brothers Shears!" and a sudden paleness overspread the usually glowing cheeks of my companion.   He was very much moved.

" I have been their friend," said he; " the poor Shears!" and he bent over the coffin, weeping.   " This one, the smallest of the two, is Henry; by his side is John, the king of men, and true type of the Irish!   Never was a soul more generous or brave.   It is he!   I know him by the length of his form.   He was six feet.   It is the one to the right, whose head is off."

And he touched the human skull.   The physiognomy was still recognisable; the lofty brow, the aquiline and prominent nose, and smiling mouth.

" As for Henry Shears, near you, he was an excellent lad, distinguished only for an absorbing love of his brother John. I knew them both, and frequently predicted to them what would be the result of their conspiracy."

Some new visitors arrived, and the voice of a child called the sacristan away to receive them.

" Will you wait a moment here, gentlemen," said he to us, " while I go to see what is desired of me?"

" Very well," said the Captain; and we seated ourselves upon a square stone opposite the mummies, and O'Mealy continued to talk of the brothers. " Every one in Ireland and England," said he, " knew that they organized, with poor Emmet, the conspiracy of the United Irishmen; but what is not known is the mysterious source that gave rise to this movement in the ardent soul of John, and that for a moment shook the power by which England enthralls us.

" At eighteen John Shears visited Paris. Your revolution, which marched with a giant's stride, was more violent from its rapidity. All popular phrensies have their Bacchantes.*

---

* It may be interesting to some readers who would refresh their memories concerning the pagan rites, from which the title in the text is taken, to read the following extract from the *Dublin University Magazine* :—" The Bacchii ecstasy was not merely drunkenness, but an epidemic madness, induced by long-continued dancing and gesticulation to the sound of cymbals and other noisy instruments. That the Bacchii and Corybantic phrensies were in all respects identical with the Middle Age dancing mania can hardly be doubted.

" Plutarch, in his thirteenth example of the ' Virtues of Woman,' has this graphic description of the condition of a band of Bacchantæ after one of their orgies :

" ' When the tyrants of Phocœa had taken Delphos, and the Thebans undertook that war against them which was called the Holy War, certain women devoted to Bacchus, (which they called Thyades,) fell frantic, and went a-gadding by night, and, mistaking their way, came to Amphissa, and being very much tired, and not as yet in their right wits, they flung themselves down in the market-place, and fell asleep, as they scattered up and down, here and there ; but the women of Amphissa ran forth into the market-place, fearing any indignity might be put upon them, and stood

In a stormy and tempestuous epoch woman partakes in the excitement, and exalts and keeps alive the flame. The Bacchante of your revolution was Theroigne de Mericourt; beautiful, reckless, eloquent; from the madness of sensuality she changed to that of spirituality; from the debauch of the senses to that of the soul; and in the fury of her orgies she embraced liberty to stain it. Possessed of a nervous temperament, which bordered on insanity, she by a certain charm drew others within her circle; without consideration, reason, or modesty, Pythoness of social destruction, seducing from the brilliancy of her Oriental beauty, and carrying all before her from her blind impetuosity, this woman John Shears saw and loved. After alluring many to their destruction, that she might obtain support in her vicious tendencies, she then availed herself of her beauty only to create fanatics. She made John Shears, that beautiful young man, who was distractedly in love with her, swear that he would shed for liberty the last drop of his blood. This fair-haired youth was seen following her, when, with dishevelled raven locks, and armed with a spear, she led to Versailles the crowd of

---

silently round about them, neither would they offer them any disturbance while they slept ; but when they were awake they attended their service particularly, and brought them refreshments; and, in fine. by persuasion, obtained leave of their husbands that they might accompany them to bring them in safety to their own borders. As for the Bacchanalian motions, and frisking of the Corybantes,' says Plutarch, ' there is a way to allay these extravagant transports by changing the measure from the trochaic to the spondaic, and the tone from the Phrygian to the Doric ;' just as with the dancers of St. Vitus and those bit by the tarantula."

her Thyades. With her he took part in the siege of the Bastile; then she forced him to enroll himself in the army of the North. He was wounded upon the field of battle; and, as a chevalier of ancient Europe, the poor boy, under the spell of the sorceress, plead for her hand as a guerdon. John Shears, who was then twenty, would absolutely marry the Bacchante. She refused. 'You may be my lover,' answered she, 'but not my master; I am predestined to liberty.' 'Ah! indeed!' cried the unhappy youth, 'we will have no bonds if you choose not, but only assure me that you love me.' 'I belong,' she replied, 'to all the lovers of liberty.'

"At one time Shears heard that Theroigne and Chenier had gone out together to attend the orgies of liberty. She came back toward midnight. The poor madman pointed to a loaded pistol which he had laid upon the table. 'See,' said he, 'to what you have reduced me, Theroigne.' She went up to the table, took the pistol, and let fly the trigger, saying—'Coward that you are, and base soul! Shame on you, to occupy yourself with a woman, instead of thinking of the Republic. Begone immediately, or I shall kill you. I shall never be yours.'

"He obeyed, and set out for Ireland, never seeing her again. I saw him then. He had written to me all the details which I recount to you.

"It was 1795. Our unhappy country was in greater turmoil and confusion than she had been for thirty years. I will not repeat to you the history of the Irish conspiracy; for the annals would re-open the fount of all our miseries. John

Shears, from temperament and opinions, from his bravery, independence, and long revolutionary education, was a redoubtable conspirator. Soon, carried along by his zeal, a multitude of inconsiderate and brave spirits took the oath of the Association. Some English spies gained admittance to one of their meetings. Henry Shears, whom his brother had initiated into the plot, and who was a weak and indiscreet man, confided to a traitor who had insinuated himself into his confidence the secret of the Association. All was now lost. The conspirators were arrested in their assembly, and incarcerated in the dungeons of Dublin. Curran, a celebrated orator, whom our country places by the side of Burke and Sheridan, was counsel for the two brothers Shears. Then was manifested the noble and generous soul of John. He thought only of saving his brother and taking the guilt upon himself, though Henry had ruined his hopes and brought him into this situation. Allowed to speak in his own defence, his pleading was an eloquent appeal to the judges for his brother, led away, said he, *by his example, and innocent of any intention, as well as any act, of sedition.* They both perished, the feeble man and the energetic man, upon the same scaffold, erected before the King's Prison.* Ah! what a soul was that of John Shears! And why was it that at eighteen years of age he should encounter that demon, torch in hand, under the guise of a woman! My friend," continued the Captain, "have a care! The first woman whom we love

---

* Prison in Dublin, so called.

decides our destiny for life : in Rousseau one sees the vulgar sensuality of Madame de Warens ; and the actresses that Lord Byron paid court to in his youth, left their stamp and impress upon his future career, which was one of foppery, ennui, and despair.

"When John Shears died with the name of Theroigne, the Bacchante was actually mad. I discovered her at the time of the peace of Amiens in one of the cells of Charenton. Near her, in an apartment elegantly adorned, dwelt another child of our sophistical epoch, M. de Sade, confined there by Napoleon. These execrable products of the eighteenth century were placed near by, and sometimes the superintendent of the hospital would make them dine together ; one, professor of the atheism of d'Helvetius, which he pushed to the extreme, the other intoxicated with the revived paganism which Mably and Anacharses had introduced to the world in Paris : two fanatics who understood each other very well, as the director of the hospital told me. The negation of God had brought back the libertine gentleman to the obscene rites of Heliogabalus, and the blasèe courtesan to the orgies of the Corybantes. Pity the young and unfortunate John Shears, who loved his country ardently, and whom this woman precipitated towards the gulf into which his brother plunged him. There is no history more deplorable. See these two brothers thrown as criminals into the trunk of an oak rudely hollowed out, and of which the law adjudged the dimensions."

Such was the narrative of my Irish friend, during which

the sacristan, who had returned, deposited his lantern near the two brothers, and remained tranquilly seated upon the earth, which would soon cover his obscure remains. Afterwards, as his turn for speaking came, making the sign of the cross, he continued his strain of panegyric, dwelling upon the sanctity of the place and the constant miracle operating there, thanks to the intervention of St. Michael.

From chemical analysis, this marvel is discovered to proceed from the absence of all aqueous particles and the constant dryness of the walls, which are stuccoed with carbonate of lime and argillaceous earth; the ground, impregnated with the same substances, absorbs the humidity and neutralizes putrid effluvia. The animal substances deposited in this cemetery, instead of decaying, dry; flesh and bone change their nature; one becomes like parchment, the other bleached, without softening, and the proportions of the corpses remain the same.

Some of the lateral chapels, which are closed by grates, contain mausoleums of many noble families. From the depths of one of these depositories of the dead, I saw a glittering light, which proceeded from two or three coronets laid upon the coffins—heraldic symbols of baronets and counts. The metal shone as if the workman had polished it the night before. The sacristan informed us that for five or six years no person had entered those chambers of the dead; and, to prove the truth of his assertion, he passed the lantern along the grate that we might see the walls covered with a tissue of spiders' webs which spread over the coffins; they filled a space four feet deep and eight broad. This enormous canopy, woven by some thousands of generations of insects, seemed a sort of mockery of the grandeur of the mausoleums.

When we came out of this little church, O'Mealy said to me, "You are, I believe, the first Frenchman who has visited these burial places ; as for the English and Germans, they never fail. The Northern populations love the dead ; but with the people of the South the sentiment and feeling of life is all-absorbing. A Grecian tomb is always concealed beneath flowers, and in some of the Antilles, every interment is the occasion of a festival, and is followed by a ball. You, charming French, you decorate your graves with all the finery and frippery of a coquette. When, for the first time, I ascended a charming hill which commanded a beautiful view of Paris, I saw gleaming in the rays of your bright sun a crowd of monuments in the form of obelisks, statues, columns, cippes, spires, altars, busts, temples, pyramids, and domes of marble. This was Père la Chaise. Even in your Parisian catacombs, the contrast between the puerile labours of man and the eternal work of death, which in her constant destruction is for ever re-creating, such exaggerated and finical display seems absurd. These fantastic tricks with human wrecks resemble a melodrama enacted by the side of Eternity. I abhor this ranging and dressing out of bones and skeletons, these myriads of classed tibias, arranged, classed symmetrically, as if to decorate a shop-window and attract the gaze of passengers. Your ancestors of the time of Louis the Sixth, your people of the League, of the party of

7*

Burgundy, or your ancestral devotees, your jolly citizens, you force them to lay their bones together as if for theatrical decoration, so much are you deluded by a taste for display."

I answered the good O'Mealy only by approving monosyllables. These ideas were very different from those which had nurtured my early years. I reflected deeply upon the dead by whom I was surrounded ; the unsightly dead with their black skins ; monks and abbesses; assassins and drunkards ; political victims ; brave men and cowards'; whose bones only served to support generations of sacristans. The dead survived their epitaphs ; the coffins were reduced to dust around their proprietors ; in fine, a poor imbecile showman drones his lullaby in our ears, perpetually repeating his traditional eulogies before the mummies, who are powerless to deny them.

Thoughts upon Ireland.

A T the commencement of the seventeenth century, when the envoy from one of the small kings of Erin presented himself before James I., dressed in a suit of woollen cloth, the ceremonial costume, all the entreaties of his chamberlains could not induce him to sleep in a bed—he preferred lying in the ashes in the chimney-corner.

The system pursued by England towards Ireland since the reign of Elizabeth has been that of cupidity, avarice, and bigotry. I am not one who can take sides with oppressors ; the right of the strongest is the right of Cain ; and I admit no more the right of cunning, commonly the strength of the weak. The scorn of England for Ireland aggravated itself to hatred in the time of Cromwell, when the savage Catholics of the last fought furiously against their heretical masters. From 1620 to 1830, Calvinism the most intolerant has been, as is well known, the pivot of English policy, and the iniquities of Great Britain towards the neighbouring isle sprung from religious hatred and Calvinistic intolerance more than aggressive power. At this day she is suffering from retributive justice. She endeavours to free herself from her turbulent neighbours ; and even Protestants fill their ill-rigged vessels with Irish Papists, in tattered shreds and half famished, to shift for themselves in the New World. In 1847 three hundred thousand Irish Catholics quitted their natal isle to seek bread or death in the United States. The new cities of North America are filled with these unhappy wretches, who not only increase the already formidable power of a rival nation, but disseminate the contagion of their hatred.

Now that the anti-Papist panic is subsiding in England, she would inculcate morals to this too long neglected race, which is devoid of principle, and the scourge of her tyrants. In vain do the English give bread to the *troublesome* Irish : as soon as the poor comprehend that alms are a salvo to keep the peace, they become more idle and poor. " We cannot," said the *Limerick Chronicle*, of August, 1846, " procure reapers. Our people had rather beg upon the high road, or implore aid from the parish, than work. It is in vain that since last Wednesday the most beautiful spires of wheat greet our eyes upon all sides, bowing their heads from their glorious loads ; there is no hand to gather and no sickle to mow them. In one week we may lose the whole harvest. It is impossible to tear this people away from the pleasures of begging or the enjoyment of their tatters. When they have suffered enough to get over the novelty, they with their quantum of potatoes embark for America, but much more for the object of seeing the country than to escape famine."

When the Irish judge that the alms proffered are insufficient, or that labour, when they accept it, is too hard, they gather together in revolt, burning and pillaging all before them. It is thus that England is punished for the education she has given her wild young sister.

Ireland has the same characteristics, both in her higher and lower classes, in the country and in the city. Dublin, which I visited with O'Mealy, is the capital least resorted to of any in Europe, but it is as motley and incongruous as all other parts of the island. You meet occasionally with equipages as splendid as those of London or Vienna, but some quarters are filled with the famished population of which I have spoken. There are cellars peopled with knaves and beggars, a motley crew, more wild and grotesque than those which formerly swarmed in the Court of Miracles. From these dens the movers in sedition recruit their forces, and, for one or two shillings per head, enroll formidable battalions. The days, or rather nights, of grand assembly, when a chief is to be elected, or the disorderly troops to be trained, they suspend, in front of their *lair* or *den* of rendezvous, a transparency which represents a half-moon, that lights the interior ; this venerated sign prohibits the access of the profane. In the mean while, balls, club-meetings, horse-racing, and all sorts of extravagances, abound ; intrigues, conspiracies cease not, and this most interesting race are forgetting themselves in the labyrinths of Parisian luxury, and endeavouring to keep at bay the inroads of grief.

My good friend, O'Mealy, said that he would initiate me into this extraordinary world, and introduce me to some individuals, fair samples of the Irish character, for an age of theories was not worth a day's observation in familiar intercourse. He added, " I will show you some types among us ; the best and the worst of these are equally bold, brilliant, shrewd, and unprincipled. There is the jovial priest, Martin Doyle, a chubby-faced abbot, like those at the time of the Reform, he will appear to you in his glory at the end of a feast, when, in the name of the Virgin, and in hatred of the Saxons, he collects guineas and shillings from the well-fed guests. At the same table you will find Lanty Lawler, a jockey, who sells the government secrets to conspirators, and the projects of conspirators to the government. You will also see old Tom Heffernan, a political jockey, who traffics in consciences—an ancient friend of Lord Castlereagh's, who brought to his master the balance due for twelve votes in one morning, playing this game for his own amusement as coolly as one would take part in a game of billiards ; he was as immoral as the thief Fresney, who defrauded the rich to give to the poor. Our popular idol is, in general, some muscular gentleman twenty times ruined, whose creditors dare not molest him, always intoxicated but always clear-headed, of Herculean vigour, and a friend of the people with whom he boxes and carouses. In addition to these accomplishments, he is a great gamester, strong aristocrat, lavish in almsgiving, has no compeer at fisticuffs, is an adept in duels, and he is one whose ardour is not diminished, nor his popularity lessened, by old age. The celebrated O'Connell unites with these qualities great cunning, wisdom, and eloquence ; thanks to these qualities, O'Connell has been our king these twenty years."

I commenced, then, under the guidance of Captain O'Mealy, the amusing study of Irish character, which gave me full occupation during my three months' tour. All the personages in the motley drama, painted to the life in Irish story, passed before me. I admired the diversity and ever-shifting variety of the scenes. The remarkable contrast between the traits in character of the Scotch, Irish, and Saxon, suggested to me the permanence of race, the power of transmitted blood,—a power which preserves the Magyar and the Sclavic, the Dalmatian and the Gipsey, distinct.

Among my new Irish friends, I should particularly signalize a sub-lieutenant, who was very giddy, and whose adventures would scarcely gain credence. I have seen no person carry to such lengths variety, bravery, and heedlessness. To-day he will travel fifty leagues in a post-chaise, during a tempest, to overtake a diligence that has not started. To-morrow he will enact the part of Othello to amuse his friends, and sleep without washing the lampblack from his face ; then at six the next morning he will appear at the military review before his colonel and the whole major staff, arrayed in uniform, sword in hand, and with his face blackened as a Moor. Always in pursuit of some fair one, sure to be balked before marriage, he nearly reached his grand climacteric without forming any matrimonial ties. Constantly on the road to great success, there he always remained. His mercurial temperament exposed him to a thousand misadventures. He would throw himself into a whirlpool, expecting by some miracle to escape. Buoyant in hope, though shipwrecked to-day, he would again set sail on the morrow. This knight-errant, always in full tilt for adventures, and adoring the marvellous, this wild Irishman, was the cadet brother of my guide, Captain O'Mealy.

We met at an ordinary in Dublin where assembled some of the whims and oddities of the place. Refinement, indolence, giddiness, coarseness, luxury, poverty, mad folly, were collected ; individuals of all descriptions, originals of every variety, met in this little corner of Europe, placed out of the sphere of English commerce and aristocratical splendours. I saw officers who had only served in Mexico ; priests who would bet and race ; coquettes who would pass for nuns ; canonesses who played the devil ; and learned men more versed in the Celtic than the English tongue. There, also, I became acquainted with a certain Doctor O'Driscol, a friend of Charles O'Mealy, the cadet, a doctor who had not, I believe, his match upon the earth.

At thirty-five, O'Driscol was always playing off some joke more worthy of Figaro than the gravity looked for in his profession ; in the mean time, he was courteous, brave, sensible ; he chattered like a magpie, was fertile in stories of all sorts, spoke not a word of truth in his gay moods, nor uttered falsity in his grave ones. With his five feet, round figure, jocund air, red, chubby cheeks, frizzled hair, and lively repartee, he was such an adept in surgery that his fellow-citizens availed themselves of his skill, and found him a very useful witness in their duels, and eight days would not pass away without his attendance being requested in an affair of honour. Resolved to amuse himself in every way, he claimed descent from Ulysses, (*Odysseus*,) of whose name, said he, *O'Driscol* was only an altered form. He never appeared except clothed in black, and never uttered a syllable that was not followed by shouts of laughter from men, or rather men-children, around. Lever has painted him under the name of Finucane.

It is well known that the Irish duel is no sham affair; fight to the death is the true Irish motto, and a duel is an every-day occurrence, thought no more of than dining out in the city. The trade of O'Driscol was to repair the arms and legs injured by this custom. One evening when we came into the smoky atmosphere of the saloon of which I have spoken, towards nine—

"From whence come you, Doctor?" called out at once two or three voices at the moment he entered, covered with dust, into the room where we were taking tea.

"What new fun have you for us?"

"Life is sad," cried the Doctor in the most easy and disengaged tone. "Poor O'Flaherty, an officer whom you have all seen frequently, has died of a wound given him by Curzon. I have attended him three days; it was impossible to save him."

These words were followed by a general lamentation—spontaneous offering to the manes of the defunct.

"He had drank so many bottles of claret! Managed a horse so well! He was so jovial withal; and adroit in *treasury business,* and could arrange affairs to the complete satisfaction of debtors !"

Then the adventures of O'Flaherty were recounted, which was a legend without an end.

" Apropos to adventures," cried Charles O'Mealy, " you doubtless know that I have been sharer in heroic honours with O'Driscol.

" No, no!" exclaimed all the company, " tell us, Lieutenant, tell us. Take a cup of tea, and let us hear."

". It is not too much to my advantage, and you will perhaps laugh at me. I permit the ladies to laugh, from homage to their sex; as to these gentlemen, that is a different thing; —they know me."

" Keep it up, Lieutenant. God bless you! This duel that now impends will be the twentieth on your own account."

" It will make my ninety-second on account of others," averred the Doctor, rising. " Speak, my dear O'Mealy."

" My adventure, then, occurred in 1839. At that time, thanks to the combats between the Orange boys and their enemies, the balls whizzed from one end to the other of the Green Isle. I was summoned by a friend, dwelling at Nais, who had an affair of honour. There was not a moment to lose. I was in Dublin when I received the letter, and had only time to run to the hotel to secure the mail-coach, with my little valise under my arm. Alas! the coach had gone! To fail in friendship was impossible—you know me. Behold me, then, in a driving tempest, with my valise and umbrella, rolling over the roads in a post-chaise, (such roads!) swearing at the postillion till we reached the little village of Konoby, where the mail-coach halted. I recognised the old driver at a glance; his broad-brimmed hat soaked in the rain, and the water spouting from its rim, with his red face half buried in an enormous cravat of the same colour. He was endeavouring to warm himself before the fire of the hostelry when he saw me, and said:

" ' Do you go with us, sir ? This is an abominable storm, and it will last. Do you calculate upon a seat outside ?'

" 'Outside ! What do you mean ? How many passengers have you inside ?'

" ' Only one ; he is a queer sort of a being, the funniest chap you ever saw. He has asked me a hundred times if I should have any other passenger. His eye is restless, his face yellow as saffron. I believe he is ill.'

" ' Know you his name ?'

" ' No. He has no luggage ; only two gray paper packets, without label or direction. He will not lose sight of them ; indeed he secures them with a tight grasp.'

" I deliberated as to passing the night with one of those disagreeable beings who sacrifice to their convenience or caprices all the comforts of others. After all, as the rain fell in torrents, and the coach was excellent, this neighbourhood of ill-humour would only be an unfortunate accessary in my stormy tour, and I took my seat rather reluctantly, I confess, in the mail-coach. The first thing I stumbled against were the legs of my fellow-passenger.

" ' Will you allow me, sir, to pass you ?' He replied not ;

but leaning towards the driver, who was shutting the door. he muttered :

" ' What the devil does he come here for ; I took my precautions.'

" ' He followed us in a post-chaise,' said the driver.

" He closed the door quickly, and the coach rolled along.

" The stranger growled, and turned his back towards me ; I was perplexed at his silence and obstinacy, and endeavoured to overcome it, and enter into conversation.

" ' This is horrible weather,' said I. In reality it hailed, and the rain beat against the glasses of the coach door.

" ' Horrible !' muttered the man, without turning.

" ' Shocking road !'

" ' Very bad; and I take care never to risk it without arms.'

" Saying this, the stranger made a movement, and I heard a clattering of arms, which seemed to proceed from a packet near him.

" This gentleman seems to possess a belligerent spirit, thought I ; and after some minutes, falling into a slumber from fatigue, I veered this way and that in such a manner as to fall upon the left shoulder of my neighbour.

" ' I have an important packet there,' he said to me ; and thrust me off very rudely ; ' you will oblige me if you will move off from it.'

" I drew back, without speaking, and in moving I shook out a little pistol that I always carried in my pocket, and it fell into my companion's lap, who trembled. ' Devil ! you are armed also !'

" ' I never go without arms.'

" ' I divined it,' sighed the unknown, giving a long, deep groan.

" I comprehended nothing of all this, and was quite perplexed at the bearing of my companion, who after some minutes began to groan anew, as if in great anguish.

" I again attempted to converse : ' You are ill, sir ?'

" ' Yes ! They know me in the country round. Ah ! if you knew to whom you spoke.' And he again sighed.

" ' I feel for you, my dear sir, though you are a stranger. I am afflicted that you should be ill in so uncomfortable a situation,—in a carriage, away from home and kind friends.'

" ' Oh, oh ! What has befallen me ? God knows ! God knows ! I am Barney Covyle, sir !'

" ' Very well, sir.'

" ' Have you not read the journals ? You must be a stranger in the country ; they are filled with my case. I have passed eighteen weeks in the hospital of Dr. Berry, and six in the great hospital, but it has done me no good.'

" ' Indeed !' replied I. I began to fear for the sanity of my fellow-traveller.

" ' Alas ! sir, if you knew who I was, you would not be very willing to travel with me.'

" ' But this was a pleasure I had not looked forward to.'

" ' Pleasure if you will have it so. When I bit the thumb of poor Thomas Owen, that did not give him great pleasure, I believe.'

" ' Bite a thumb ?' asked I, trembling, and sinking down to the floor of the carriage ; ' and for what ?'

" ' Ah !   Why ! why !   They are not agreed upon that. Some say it is the liver, others the brain ; these, that it is the spine; those, the pericardium ; as for me, I believe they are all wrong alike.'

" ' Is there a name for your malady ?'

" ' Alas ! there is.'

" ' What ?'

" ' I do not like to say. If I was to have a paroxysm of the phrenzy, this night—but I will endeavour to keep it off.'

" ' How! such attacks! and they suffer you to take a seat in the coach when you are in this condition ?'

" ' Ah! they know it not.   I am sure old Rowney barks and howls now, wretched dog that he is.'

" ' Rowney ?'

" ' Yes, the dog that bit me.

" ' Ah, ah ! Is this disorder of yours called hydrophobia ?'

" ' Exactly.'

" There was silence; during which I scarcely breathed, but remained trembling in all my members, and looking at the carriage-door; the horses travelled at a quick pace.   My mad companion continued :

" ' It is only eight days since I began to bite;' this he said with imperturbable gravity; ' I am in my good moments.'

" ' But you ought never to have come out,' said I, elevating my voice.

" ' Speak not so loud, I pray you, that excites me.'

"'Sir,' I said, in a tone soft and gentle, 'it is imprudent for you to be travelling in this condition.'

"'Oh! if I should not see a river, a fountain, nor running water of any sort, I can go on. It is the water, sir, that I cannot endure. That brings on my paroxysms.'

"The coach rapidly reached the bridge of Leighlin, and I, as may be easily believed, felt fear creeping through every pore. My eye fixed upon my terrible companion, watching fearfully all his movements, my ear catching his faintest breath, I cursed the hour, the folly, and the post-chaise, which had plunged me into this absurd and cruel danger. At length I heard him snore. 'Is this a precursory symptom of the access of his disease!' thought I. Hastening to avail myself of his slumber, I gently reached my hand to the sash of the door, slowly and softly letting it slide down, drawing out my legs by degrees from under the seat, I finished by slowly opening the door, and glided noiselessly down the steps into the muddy road; then with a stentorian voice I cried out to the driver: 'Stop! I wish to get up upon your coach.' The tempest was more violent than ever. The driver was much surprised to see a young man in a frock-coat, without any outside garment, exposing himself in such a storm. At last, shivering and benumbed with cold, I stopped with the carriage at the hotel Trefle, at Nois.'

"Whatever satisfaction I felt in escaping from the hydrophobe, I was urged on by curiosity to see what became of my insupportable fellow-traveller, and determined, if necessary, to set the police upon his track. I let myself down lightly, and I saw the hydrophobe with his packets under his arm, which no doubt contained his arms, stepping most peaceably into the hotel.

" ' Stop that man !' I cried to the driver.

" ' Stop whom ?'

" ' The madman in the green surtout.'

" In the mean time, the hydrophobe laid down his two packets on the table in the inn, and, peaceably removing his outside garment, he warmed his feet. Three or four handkerchiefs of wool and silk which guarded his throat, and half muffled his face, were successively removed; and when followed by the crowd, who were aghast, I entered the hotel, the hydrophobe, turning round, hailed me :

" ' Ah! friend, how have you been since we dined together ? I had not recognised you, nor you me, I think,—had you ?'

" ' How! Is this you, Dr. O'Driscol, who have been playing the harlequin at my expense, making me pass the night in the battery of a storm ?'

" ' A word in thine ear, friend,' said O'Driscol, with a mysterious air; ' seest thou these two little packets ? They contain fifty thousand pounds sterling, intrusted to my care by young Nelson, who was killed in a duel before my eyes. I was alone in the coach; it was known I was carrying money; I took thee, friend, for a thief, and rid myself of thy company as I best could.' "

These whimsical frivolities amused me much at the time. I was too young to read the riddle of the sphynx, and perceive the reality behind the veil. During this charming sport, balls flew, houses were burned, the peasantry killed and mutilated each other. There was no well-being; heroism everywhere, good sense nowhere. The drama unfolded, and yet life was not serious. The people conspired to relieve themselves from ennui, and assassinated a neighbour to pass away time. Every thing conspires against poor Ireland. Even her peculiar geographical position, and her recklessness, continually place her in imminent peril. Over-excitement has become necessary to the people. Their whole life is a drama. They are continually contriving little scenes whose only purpose is frolic. In Ireland, as in France, the masses are theatrical; they love decoration and costume; they also follow instinct, but fail in principle.

I had seen in England hard and rebellious spirits, pliable under the law, and contributing to the grandeur and glory of the nation; but in this country justice is no longer respected. At the assizes, when the list of the accused was larger than ordinary, and the people interested themselves in some among them, the military force was called out to secure the prisoners; then the village became a camp. Many of the neighbouring hamlets would assemble to lend their aid, and united they would all rush upon the troops to tear from justice the unfortunate victims. Soon women and children mingle in the combat; the streets are filled with the wounded and dying, and houses are often burned during the affray. At length the justice of peace, who had formerly been a conspirator, but becoming discontented with his accomplices, had betrayed them in good season to secure him-

8

self life and the recompense of office, passes sentence upon the offenders with all the cruelty of a renegade.

No delineator has drawn to the life, no historian has reproduced, the Irish; their mad freaks and sudden ebullitions; their burlesques and chaotic straining after the impossible. Ireland is certainly a unique country.

I would not let O'Mealy rest until he had arranged a tour that I wanted to take with him along the Irish coasts and through the richest districts of that unhappy country. The landscapes of Ireland resemble no others; an expression of melancholy and solitary wildness pervades them. The cragged and sharp outlines of the mountains assume anomalous forms, and give you an impression of strange and almost grotesque wildness. There seems to have been in times past a frolic of Nature ; the wild sports of her giant rocks, if I may so say. But Nature's freaks are most perceptible amid the solemn and heavy superincumbent granite blocks: whenever she detects a flaw or cavity in these old fixtures, she fills it with a soft mould, and up springs a garden of gay colours; scarlet-broom, and other flowers, intermingled with the deep verdure of the fern. Upon the sides of the rocky hills issue a thousand little streams, which in their sinuous path sometimes creep, and then again rush foaming over the innumerable little angles and edges which offer obstruction to their course; and at length, after tumbling and foaming in sparkling jet-d'eaux, they reunite in the hollow of a valley, seeming to bemoan their imprisonment. All along the coast are glens and ravines, many leagues in length, where you

meet no living beings except sheep, without shepherds. The
unceasing moan of the winds, the lengthened murmur of the
waves, the savage wildness of the peasants' huts, half concealed by the scraggy branches of the scarlet-oak, added still
to the desolateness of the scene. It seemed impossible that
human beings could be sheltered by these bits of granite-
stones, heaped up without cement, or that they could content
themselves within their mud-walls and thatched roofs, which
have cost but ten shillings in erecting. Upon the summit of
an ocean promontory, I saw the outlines of a child watching
one or two nanny-goats; his figure, almost denuded, seemed
sketched upon the cerulean blue of the heavens. He was
singing some old Gaëlic air, of which he knew not the meaning. Since his birth he has seen only the clouds which flit
across the heavens, the will-o'-wisps from the marsh, and one
or two rude cabins ; all his lore is the superstitious legends
instilled by his mother. The extent of his knowledge of
civilization is, that down below is a little chapel, and farther
along, between two crags, is a thatched cabin, of which the
back is a granite-rock, and its sign waves in the breeze and
swings in the storm. This *remarkable* building is a *shebeen*,
or tavern, seldom visited except by smugglers, and whose
only room is at the same time a kitchen and a parlour, a
dining-hall and a sleeping-apartment. There the smugglers
halt, and recreate themselves by cursing the Saxons, and
seeking means to fight them. Frequently a subterranean
gallery, excavated within the rocks, serves as a receptacle
for barrels of brandy, small bales of lace, fusils, and powder,

to sell in the interior, or to such persons as foment the periodical insurrections of the country. The landlady of the smuggler's inn, of pure Irish race, would be slain sooner than betray her accomplices, who are sailors, pirates, jockeys, and refugees from justice; these are all united by a common hatred against England.

> "The Irishman is worth his weight in gold,
> And the Saxon the gallows is just fit to hold."

This refrain, reduced some ages since from two Gaëlic verses, and sang in chorus by the whiskey revellers in the *shebeen*, still echoes from one end of Ireland to the other. You hear it in the streets of Dublin, and in the midst of the bogs which cover the central part of Ireland ; it is the concrete of the national sentiment, the indelible thought of Ireland, and her whole political code.

If you proceed some leagues farther, and gain admittance into a feudal château, you will see two square towers and battlements, which were formerly united to a wall, now destroyed. You will there find the same characteristics ; the same animosity, in its rash and furious impotency, against the stranger and the Saxon. All their miseries, moral and material, are displayed upon a great scale ; a shattered manor, disorderly farm, and fortress in ruins. This singular château is open to the winds on all sides. All you see manifests negligence and inveterate idleness. A forest of lawless elms obtrude their branches through the broken parapets. One or two little structures, with pyramidal roofs, and covered

with tiles of broken slate, are attached to the main building.
Ploughs in a ruinous condition, and rusty harrows, were
thrown pell-mell in the midst of armorial escutcheons and
broken ogives ; sheep, oxen, and fox-hounds saunter lazily
down broken terraces which descend to the sea; the basins
and fish-ponds are half choked up by parasitical plants, which
spread afar their putrid miasmas.   In fine, if you enter
under the vault, you pass through a large court, meeting
no other obstruction than broken flag-stones, brambles, and
falling stones from the walls.   Passing along through large
desert corridors, doors opening to the right and left, you see
solitary unfurnished apartments.   The family, who bear a
name more ancient than that of de Coucy, have sought
refuge in a tower, half ruined.   There they live, *sans nul
pensement*, as said La Fontaine, upon the wrecks of glory.
The fire blazes in the large chimney ; frequently the echoes
of their orgies mingle with the murmurs of the neighbouring
ocean.   The gouty patriarch, whose embroidered and faded
vest has seen better days, and whose eyes sparkle beneath a
crown of silvered curling locks, is not the last to curse the
Saxon.   Half peasant and half gentleman, he is attired in
black woollen stockings, old breeches of tawny velvet, buckles
which simulate the diamond, ruffles in the style of Louis
XV., coat and vest "à la Française."   He has passed his
life in selling cheap and buying dear, and has "burned the
candle at the two ends," as said Panurge.   His youngest
son, lieutenant of the horse, and his eldest, who will inherit
his title, follow in the same path.   The patrimony having

entirely disappeared, they have no more care, and it is a hundred to one if they do not conspire against their oppressors.　Although the real ownership of the domain and ruined château may be an hypothesis, and it has been subjected to mortgage upon mortgage for at least six generations past, still no usurious creditor has ever dared to rout the family and take possession.　The vassals (as poor as the lord of the manor) would drive off invaders with the fusil or club.　Should necessity or chance lead an Englishman to these desert shores, no one would point out his path; swarms of tattered beggars would surround him, weeping or laughing, and asking alms ; and the poorest mountain peasant would receive a better welcome than the Saxon stranger.

In returning through the central parts of the island, you find yourself amid the bogs, more desolate and sad than the scenery of rock, hill, and shore, you have quitted.　Proceeding farther, you see a large extent of country, and many tanneries scattered along; you meet with multitudes of living animals, that seem like beasts upon two legs, nearly denuded, and midway between intoxication and famine— between the slumber of the brute and sanguinary combat.

O'Mealy said to me, in his prelude to my tour:· "When you have studied the origin and progress of our miseries, material and moral, you will no more rely upon the sayings of the philosophers and politicians.　In Ireland, all that the English esteem is scorned ; and the reverse holds true. Enter one of our thatched cabins, without roof, door, or chimney, the walls half covered with remnants of old garbs, and there you will see squeezed together five or six poor wretches, almost as naked as their asylum, partaking of their bread that was baked six months since, and must be cut with a hatchet. You will find that this family of men, women, and children, seated upon their damp clay floor like beasts in their lair, devouring ill-cooked potatoes, the only luxury for festival-days, not only feel no envy of the small proprietors ·of English farms, who rise at five in the morning, and gain their living by the sweat of the brow, but they would regard them as vile slaves. And, in fact, the Saxon, who calls himself free, is a slave, from labour and habit. The poor Celt of our bogs is free as the roamer of the woods. The layer above is of the same mould ; full of giddy independence, the frequenters of concerts, theatres, and balls. You will understand the significance of the plaintive and wild melodies of Thomas Moore. Sometimes you hear, mingling with tramp of dancing and gaiety of music, groans from rebels flogged under the Governor's window.

" The subdivisions of our small farms into still smaller portions, which will scarcely maintain the occupants, are the material causes of the ruin of the country.

" The English or Irish proprietor of twelve thousand acres, would fear to live in a country where the smallest farmer or tenant, who was discontented with his lot, might waylay him in the corner of a wood, or behind a hedge, with a pistol or club. He would take no care of his domain, but leave it to the administration of the *middle-man*, (an agent who pays him the rent,) and spend in other countries the revenue accruing to him. In his absence, the land would be divided and subdivided as the middle-man found it for his interest; and the portions, already so small, the renters would let out to others, till the whole would swarm with miserable wretches, who multiply in proportion to their distress : true warren of wild animals, of which each one in ordinary times could scarcely live by cultivating his one or two inches, and the first year of dearth, fever, and famine would carry off thousands." The Captain continued his description as having been an eye-witness : "When I visited Donegal, I perceived plainly that the more the land was divided, the more miserable were the peasants. At Raphoe, especially, extreme misery had reduced men and women to the condition of skeletons, and many of the people kept their beds, not having clothes to wear. This frightful life has its charms for our poor savages ! They taste, in their independence, a ferocious joy that they would not exchange for any rational liberty. You might deprive them of life sooner than the hand-breadth of soil which is their pride, although it ruins, instead of supporting them."

Upon our return to Dublin, I asked Captain O'Mealy if he hoped that Ireland would ever emerge from barbarism.* His answer was, that " Political formulas would never suf-

---

* Many of the ideas in this Essay upon Ireland, of which a part appeared in 1848, are precisely those that the great statesman, Sir Robert Peel, endeavoured to enforce; also Sir John Russell, in 1849. It seems indubitable that they would save Ireland.

fice, or special parliament of their own. Brilliant metaphors
—bold apostrophes—would rush upon us, from their eloquent
speeches, as cataracts; neither would they fail in the spirit
of intrigue, more than in order and eloquence ; but Ireland
would gain nothing thereby. Ireland resembles the child
who would withdraw itself from the family shelter, and cannot prosper alone or separated ; independent spirits who, to
gratify vanity, would compromise life itself. The vital interest of Ireland is to remain united to the family group
which composes Great Britain. A government of her own
would not suit the habits of this people. To attain that,
she is lacking in every suitable quality, and even defective.
She has no patience, perseverance, economy, and love of
labour; she poorly cultivates her soil, and has not the taste
to cultivate it well; she unites the Indian's want of foresight
to the taste for luxuries and splendours of civilized life.
Peasants, citizens, lords, love extravagance, and even ruin;
a quiet and calm life would be an insupportable burden ;
they would not give a day of idleness and revelry, combats
and adventures, for ten years of the riches of Holland, ensured by a life of industry. The civilizer, or rather, the
restorer, of Ireland, would have to struggle against the useless virtues and brilliant qualities of this extraordinary race.
He would have to redeem a soil let alone for ages, and
become a stagnant morass.*

---

* Here follow some details upon the resources of Ireland, her commerce, and the banking system, which might not interest the general
reader.

8*

"But the moral metamorphosis is above all things necessary. How proceed to labour in mines and drain land, when one part of Ireland would not suffer the introduction of foreign workmen, and another is too proud to labour? How obtain the capital necessary, if it is thought dishonourable and degrading to use the hatchet and spade, the shovel and mattock? If our indolent race is appalled at the idea of burning heaths, draining morasses, applying the water-power to manufactures, exploring mines of copper and coal, the exercise of political rights more extended would prove a weariness to the flesh.

"It would be a sublime work to civilize Ireland. She offers the most beautiful elements to encourage the attempt: a common faith; a race, keen, shrewd, intelligent, and brave. Whoever lends himself to the great mission, should take warning from the materialists of France, and before proceeding to re-organize Ireland, and promote her material interests, should begin at the source, and revive the divine idea of moral perfection."

In this, my first tour in Ireland, I descried in the distant horizon that little cloud, slowly arising, which burst in a tempest at the crisis of 1847, when there was not only a famine, but a revolt—prelude to the catastrophes which befell Europe in 1848. Ireland was in the vanguard of our miseries; she sent forth the savage war-whoop before the battle. She suffered more keenly than we in France from the same evils: social iniquities, a population without principle, and without bread; sensual materialism, giving an imperfect civilization and a false education; barbarism, springing from the bosom of corruptions; an ill division of labour and capital; above all, great crimes from a people over-excited by the horrors of famine. If I speak thus freely of this charming and afflicted race, whom I have seen so intimately, it is because the vices which are destroying them are ours. With Ireland, as with us, the question that is called political is altogether moral. Restore health and activity to these proud and jealous souls, and they will take care of the rest. Instil religion and morality, and you will see these bright intelligences reconstruct society. It is in vain to give them formulas. Examine the grievances of France for a hundred years past, and you will perceive that formulas or political constitutions, new organizations without end, and prescriptions which cannot be followed, do not reach the depth. Unless you could change the men, you cannot prevent the peasant from preferring death in hunger and rags, and the pleasure of fighting his neighbour when drunk, to living respectably and industriously under a slated roof, and cultivating his own field. Labour is a hard thing; economy induces weariness; go and propose to this people to pursue these virtues, and be recompensed by order, neatness, and comforts—*this people*, who for five hundred years have revelled in the perils and pleasures of savage life, and they would spurn your counsel.

The genius of Ireland offers the most singular *mélange* that the migration of races, in their various stages of culture or ignorance, has ever produced. Celts, Milesians, thrown by political chances into a Teutonic-Anglo-Norman frame, they have preserved their Oriental indolence, subject to terrible outbreaks, with the old Celtic rapidity of action. Like us, they pass quickly from thought to act. To vehemence and credulity, to the Asiatic apathy and ardour, the Irish unite the suppleness and versatility of the Celt. Love and war are necessary to them. Their political nullity and commercial inferiority drives them to revelry, which under another sun and another situation might not seduce them, but now it benumbs their sense of pain. When they cannot fight, they simulate the battle whose reality it is not in their power to enjoy. Even children, coming from school, seek occasion to assail the passengers; the people mix in the brawl, and attack or defend one another with stones.

Without end or aim for his activity, however, the Irishman remains faithful to his country; this is the beautiful side of his character. The Irish type is never obliterated; it is every where recognisable in the spheres of art, poetry, and politics. The young daughter of Ireland, with blue eyes and black hair, full of witchery and caprice, sings her national melodies, wild and sportive, joyous and melancholy, and from the slowest and most mournful ditties darts at once to the most vivacious. In fine, a meridional richness of genius is concealed beneath the barbarism of the North; a ray shines forth behind the clouds; a gleam of Oriental poetry peers through their tears, and almost irradiates their rags. Strange and sad grandeur! Even politics is a little mad in Ireland, at which no person in France has a right to be astonished; shaking her cap and bells, her great men make brilliant harangues; the reckless, giddy multitude are roused to riot, break heads, which all serves their own ruin, and the good of their enemies. But it is not for us, alas! to blame them.

Such is unfortunate Ireland.*

---

* The following remarks from an Edinburgh Review chime in so well with the comparison of Chasles between his own country and Ireland that I insert them here. Speaking of the arbitrary rule of the usurper, the reviewer says :—

"The natural result of such a tyranny is either a sudden and universal insurrection, or silent abject submission. There can be no middle course. The French have preferred the latter. They are bold, but not resolute. They are violent and impetuous, but not enthusiastic. The audacity with which the mob has, from time to time, risen against the garrison of Paris, murdered its outposts, stormed its barracks, and repulsed its assaults, is the fruit, not so much of any love of freedom or hatred of despotism, as of indifference to what they were hazarding. A life alternating between toil, vice, and debauchery, endeared by few social sympathies, ennobled by no ulterior objects, a mere struggle for existence and amusement, is readily risked, because it is scarcely worth preserving. The *émeuteur* gambles with life, as he is ready to gamble with any thing else that he possesses : if he wins he has a week or two of triumph, and boasting, and importance : if he falls, his troubles are over, and he quits a world in which he had to suffer far more than to enjoy. Such insurgents may sweep away by sudden assault an unprepared or inadequate regular force. For one day, for two days, and it may be for three, they can repel from their barricades even a considerable army, but they are unfit for a prolonged civil war They want skill, they want combination, and, above all, they want pertinacity."

Sea-shore Scenes.

THE SMUGGLERS.

WE again crossed the Channel; I parted from O'Mealy at Anglesea, and from thence returned to London. The following summer, a young man named Boyce, a poet, and in a decline, interesting and gentle, like all those who feel that life is departing, and who aspire to a better world, was going to visit his family in the little village of Nacton, county of Suffolk; and he proposed to me to accompany him. I assented with pleasure to this proposition, as I should see the coasts of England under a new point of view, and the varied scenery of the sea-shores, with the eccentricities and peculiarities of the natives, opened a new field of observation.

The little village of Nacton is not far from the ocean, and is near the confluence of the rivers Stour and Orwell, which at their embouchure form dangerous alluvions of sandbanks overgrown with grass. Between the river Orwell and Nacton there is a large tract of land, renowned to this day for its fertility, called Wolfskettel, which owes its appellation to the bloody battle fought by the Saxon duke of that name against the Danes. It would seem that human blood has a wonderful effect in fertilizing the land, or that God recompenses man by his benefactions for the grievous outrages they inflict upon each other, for almost all fields of battle, and this among others, have become celebrated for the opulence of their harvests. In the midst of an arid and desolate shore, a portion of Wolfskettel has been cultivated with success these ten ages past by a race of farmers, for the most part descendants of the Danish invaders. A large mass of yellow hair flows over the shoulders of these tall, stalwart men, with large breadth of shoulders, as you would know by seeing the hand of one of them, leaning upon the plough-horse of the North, almost as enormous as the master, who guides it in the plough from morning till night along the furrows with imperturbable gravity. The animals and men bear some resemblance to each other, for the silvered mane of the mare, and her strong withers, the large breast, and clear bay colour, harmonize with the fair hair of her leader, as it floats in the wind. The patois of these peasants is of another age and another world. The cry *whore-r-r-hie*, when they finish one furrow and begin another, recalls the old accent of war. The strong gutturals of the North, issuing from these colossal chests, are as unintelligible to the English of London as the language of the Caribbee Islands. Sometimes we see a fair-haired, fair-faced Saxon girl steering one of these horses, without saddle, her little bare legs almost hid in the horse's mane. The women also ride these unsaddled horses without fear; and in the frequent encounters of the smugglers with

the guard-posts, one frequently sees them—or rather one has
seen them, for these customs are passing away—-handle man-
fully the short-sword of the mariner, and the fusil used in
boarding a ship.   The names of their counties are as untinged
with Norman sounds as their race is unmixed with Norman
blood; (as North-folk, *Norfolk*; South-folk, *Suffolk*; East-
Saxon, *Essex*;) also their family names, Cracknell, Catchpole, Wringnell, Springtree, true commoners' names, have
descended for centuries unallied with the aristocratic nomen-
clature of Beauclerc (Beauclerck), des Couray (Churchill), of
Normandy.

The little village of Nacton, in the county of Suffolk, has
only one street, which seems to pursue its quiet way, lagging
along the edge of a dark ravine, and you ask whether this
village is alive or dead.   Traversing this deserted street in
the night, you are surprised at a low roaring sound which
follows you; that is the ocean, which you see not, but it
speaks to you, for it is near.   The city of Ipswich, built
almost at the mouth of the Orwell, is the centre of agricul-
ture and commerce of all this district of country.   The
traveller sees it when, leaving the little village of Nacton, he
reaches the summit of a hill, which is called Bishop's Hill;
one side looks upon the ocean, the other offers a rich and
extensive view of the country.   An amphitheatre unequally
wooded, where arise before you, as by stages, woods and
meadows, and you count twelve little boroughs or cities,
known by the spires of twelve Gothic churches.   Then in the
distance you perceive the serpentine Orwell, which augments

as it approaches the sea, waters many valleys, disappears, and reappears in the lights and shadows, describes an elegant curve, and, forming an arc of a circle partly around the pretty town of Ipswich, situated at the foot of the hill, rushes on over the dangerous sandbars of which I have spoken, and making a junction with the Stour, is merged in that stream. These shores have frequently been selected by English landscape painters, to whom they offer a favourite study; they can rarely find combined maritime views and rustic charms, the contrast of smiling culture and the savage wildness of a desolate coast.

During my stay in Nacton I gathered the details of a popular idyl, which I will presently relate. It arose in real life, the most low and savage; it commenced in the murmur of the roar of the German Ocean, and ended in the murmurs of the Pacific. The facts are authentic, attested by the journals of the time and the records of judicial authority. Justice, who willingly interferes with the romance of the people, was engaged largely here.

Towards the end of the last century an old superstition was attached to one of the most sterile and elevated points of the coast, called Bawdsey Cliff, which still subsisted, and seemed even to revive. The coast-guards (mostly from Ireland) were stationed at different distances, in order to watch for the embarkations of the smugglers; and in their ghost-like wanderings or concealments in dark, mysterious ravines, where they would lie in ambush, contributed not a little to maintain popular agitation; for no people are so superstitious as the Irish. In the mean time, they were active and vigilant, distinguished for their love of fighting and giddy bravery; these qualities, together with the tricks and stratagems which, like the savage, they employed, made them fearful to the enemies of custom-house duties. They braved heat and cold, wind and rain—and the fearful north winds whistled fitfully over these sands; and still more, their duties exposed them to the hatred and malevolence of the neighbourhood. But they felt no personal animosity; they would kill and be killed with imperturbable good-humour.

The friends of the smugglers would pardon those Irish coast-guards who would frequently sit at their table and relate marvellous stories : for instance, that upon the declivity of Bawdsey Cliff dwelt a legion of phantoms, which were the ghosts of smugglers of past times ; that their apparitions boded ill; that they vanished in the sands at will, and that all the officers of government hardy enough to follow them were infallibly ingulfed in subterranean regions. Listen, reader, to the cause of this belief, which, thanks to the oratory of the Irish and the credulity of their auditors, spread far and wide.

On the summit of Bawdsey Cliff was a poor rude cabin, with a little orchard enclosed by a stone wall, without cement. Near the cabin, behind the wall of the orchard, was an immense well, without curb-stone, remarkable only for the size of the cable and the wooden bucket which served to draw water. The orifice of this well was guarded by heaps of broken pottery and fragments of bottles. It was not without motive that the access was made so difficult. About twelve feet below the ground, in the side of the well, which was walled with stones and pebbles, was a small arcade, which served for an entrance to a singular grotto, that was unknown to all the country around, though it was one of the natural curiosities.

The form of this grotto is as an immense cylinder, as perfect as if constructed by square and compass. There were incontestable marks that this cave had formerly contained a mass of waters, which gradually excavated, or ploughed for itself in many concentric circles, a passage to the sea through this vault. The smugglers around this coast had long since availed themselves of this natural resource. They had turned the course of the water, and excavated a path towards the ocean; they also made a subterranean communication from their grotto to the chimney of the cabin, so that the smoke from their fire should find the same vent. In fine, that they might complete the success of so many ingenious contrivances, they had furnished, with some attempt at beauty, their domicil, where one could enter only through the well; that is to say, take passage in a bucket, and aided by the peasant or his wife, stop before the arcade which served as a doorway to the grotto. The wall concealed the well from those who ascended the cliff by the sea, so that the smugglers, keenly pursued, would wind round the wall, fling themselves into the bucket, stop at the archway by means of a grappling-iron which served them for an anchor, and there hide themselves in their

obscure retreat, where they found food, fire, and shelter.
This magical vanishment of the contrabandists had so often
recurred, that at Nacton and Ipswich it had become an
article of faith.

But there was one of the Irish coast-guards whom this
supernatural explanation would not satisfy. This man,
Patrick O'Brian, was shrewd, and determined to see into
the matter. He had remarked the wall around which the
pursued always turned, and he was filled with an intense
curiosity to look into the interior of the *Phantom's Well*.
This cost him dear, as we shall soon see.

An old labourer and his family lived in the cabin, of
whom the smugglers had made friends. Almost all the
population of these strands are poor. Many bales of
lace, more than one high-priced shawl, and innumerable
casks of brandy, rum, gin, which were called in their slang,
foam of the sea, found their way to the peasants, who had
no desire to take part against illegal industry which supplied
them with precious goods at so cheap a rate. The larger
part of the peasantry around *did not know* when the captains
of the brigs disembarked with their cargoes, which they
still call the *cargo of moonshine*. The inhabitants of these
coasts, like people of all countries, as soon as they can attest
their ancient enjoyment of the most lawless freedom, claim it
as a right; and people of the frontiers, as those of the
coasts, would willingly arm themselves against the law to
defend the contrabandists of the sea or land. The wife
of the labourer was of the same opinion, for she had re-

ceived more than *one present* to confirm it, from the captains
of the brigs, and was therefore their devoted friend. Poor
Pat, the coast-guard, therefore, could not have done a more
unwise thing than to express to one of these female partisans
his desire to see a little of what passed inside this famous
well. She consented without much urging, since he had
such a "strange fancy," to aid him. Then she assisted
him in placing himself at ease in the bucket; but the chain
unrolling with more rapidity than he expected, he was
plunged and replunged in the bottom of this well as often
as suited the woman who balanced the chain. In vain
by his plaintive cries did he endeavour to soften this female savage. "*Jwhel!* H'angel! D'harling!" exclaimed he,
with the Oriental guttural. She ceased not to ply the
cord, alternately sinking and raising her victim, till she
heard him no longer. Pat was now sensible of his fool-
hardiness, and holding fast upon the iron ring of the bucket,
he moved not. He hoped by feigning death to escape his
persecutor, and climb the length of the cable with that skill
and agility that mariners frequently exercise on shipboard.
He had an affair with bitter enemies, as adroit and more
vigilant than he. The advantage was on their side.

At length he raised his head, and hearing no sound,
looked up, called, and hearing no reply he seized the chain,
and by the aid of hands and feet soon reached the opening
in the wall of the well. At that moment, stopping to draw
breath, believing himself safe, his legs were caught by iron
pincers, which squeezed them mercilessly; his hands let go

their hold, he fell head downwards, and was drawn through
the arch into the grotto, where a mattress sheltered his poor
head, which run the risk of being broken against the wall of
the well.   In fine, he was now in the spirits' cave, and
his ears were regaled by shouts of laughter, at his expense,
which resounded from side to side ; and he saw a dozen
sailors whom the misadventures of the too curious coast-
guard had excited to extraordinary and noisy mirth.

In fact, it so chanced that Pat was introduced to the full
assembly of freebooters, however unwittingly ; and if we
had a romance to write, we should here paint the interior
of the cavern, the flaming torches, the mustachios of these
wild men, the fright of Irish Pat, and his belief that hell
had opened her yawning gulf to receive him ; but we find
nothing of all this in the *reports* and *judiciary documents* of
the year 1790, when this scene was enacted.   We say only,
and without entrenching upon the domain of romancers, that
our freebooters felt themselves as much embarrassed by their
prize as Pat by his intrusion.   There were many opinions
advanced in this assembly, but that which united the
greatest number of voices was very rigorous—nothing less
than to destroy poor Pat, as the only means to ensure
eternal silence and rid themselves of all fear.   Pat, too late,
cursed his bold and reckless curiosity; he had discovered the
secret which, if made known, would put these marauders'
lives in jeopardy, but he had put his own life in the power of
those who hesitated at no crime.   These men then prayed
the Irishman to take a glass of gin, to comfort his heart and

prepare him for his last trip, telling him he should go off in the style that suited him best. "Will you be drowned in the well, or hewn to pieces by the sabre?" said they. He replied, "I choose neither the one nor the other." Just then, as they were all in merriment, the captain entered, if we can call it an entrance, being let down in a bucket, and crawling through a hole in the wall, as before described.

Will Laud—for such was his name, and he will frequently appear in our history—was a young man of twenty-five, and recognised for chief by these men. He ordered that the eyes of the poor Irishman should be bandaged, and his face covered with a thick veil, and the chain from the well should be set a-going. Pat, who believed he should be drowned, prayed to Saint Patrick; but, instead of descending, he felt himself drawn up : and when his eyes were uncovered, he found that he was in a very pretty brig, even that of Captain Laud ; they coasted some time near the shore, and at last left him on a desert point upon the eastern shore, and giving him some money for his journey, enjoined silence as the price of the life granted.

From this account of the smugglers, it may be seen how great were the resources at their disposal, and how deep and extensive was the basis and sphere of their operations. Profiting from these favourable circumstances, and above all, from the interest they inspired amongst the larger part of the labourers and peasants, they employed spies, had their fortresses and pleasure-houses, their treasury, their marine, their arsenal, and even their relay horses. It frequently so

It was not surprising that Laud, in spite of the opposition of his father, hearkened and yielded to the seductions of this wily man.   The life of the smugglers passed for a heroic and glorious one; whilst the waves rolled over the rocks and sands, the newspapers of London and the interior every day conveyed news to these poor and ignorant rustics of battles, glory achieved, countries vanquished, riches well or ill-acquired, and all concurred to induce the inhabitants of these coasts to tempt fortune, and gain honours and riches.   A powerful motive had, above all, induced Laud to choose this perilous career; he was poor, and a lover.   He had seen and loved the young Margaret, daughter of a farmer at Nacton, named Catchpole, who was a charming girl, and she was by no means indifferent to him.   How assure to his betrothed the independence so desirable ?   The regular path of industry was long; that of the sea and contraband trade offered immediate profits.   Beginning his career, then, without warning Margaret, he accepted the brig offered him by the Captain; and from that time was continually on the route from Holland to England, and from England to Holland. He was one of the boldest and most successful of sea-robbers; and he gained renown of that sort.   " Will Laud," said the Reverend Richard Cobbold, who had known him, and would willingly excuse him, " was the true type of his race and his calling.   Brow noble, head erect, an eye of blue, hair fair and curling, Roman nose, imperious and command-ing, mouth resolute, and chin full, his countenance bespoke resolution in the face of peril, ardent love of enterprises in the mode of life which without doubt his ancestors had followed—pirates of the North, who came to this country to obtain land more fertile than their home afforded. Margaret Catchpole offered a type quite the contrary, says Cobbold : "complexion olive, and glowing with gipsey blood, hair black and straight, her dark eyes brilliant and intelligent, her cheeks full, her figure slender."

Such are the personages of this drama: vulgar, assuredly, by their condition and fortune; attractive through their contrasts, and that another destiny would have led to what men call heroism. Laud possessed bravery and generosity, as his conduct to the poor Irishman testified ; as to Margaret Catchpole, who holds the first place in this narrative, her nature was more remarkable. Give their true rank to popular energies, place in their true position each one of the sons of God, how would the human soul be honoured every where, and the individual be valued as man under any circumstances or accidents !

The resolution of William was keenly felt by Margaret, and incurred her just censure. She had always refused to receive the presents of ribbons and laces that the smugglers had urged upon her. The course of things justified the forebodings of the young maiden and proved the wisdom of her counsels, for the path William had taken was beset with dangers.

One day the ferryman from Harwich (the government had deprived Laud's father of his little post, to punish him for the sins of his son) brought news to the parent that his son's skull was terribly fractured in a scuffle. Edward Barry, head of the coast-guards upon the shore of Bawdsey, had wounded him in mortal combat. Margaret during a month watched over him, cured his wound, and made him promise that he would engage no more in such hazardous enterprises ; but William had given a promise difficult or impossible for him to adhere to. Once have a taste of the Bohemian life, upon land or water, and one is infatuated with the fatal charms of this independent, wayward course. William now quitted Nacton, where he had been so tenderly nursed by Margaret, hastened to his brig, adopted the cognomen of Captain Hudson, and continued in the same course. He found in this trick the advantage of passing for dead, and eluding Edward Barry, the coast-guard.

Barry—and this will charm the systematic spirits who hold to the theory of races—in nothing resembled William Laud. It is well known that the name of Barry is the same as the Norman Barrè, a name metamorphosed by their sojourn in England. The name proceeded from an order of friars who wore cloaks spotted with black and white. The Barrys were brave, but perfectly submissive to the laws of their country ; sworn enemies to smugglers and their habits. John Barry, brother to Edward, who fought with Will Laud, was more gentle in character and milder in manners than his brother. He was in the employ of the Alneshbourne farmer, near Margaret's home. He loved Margaret. The character of *Ralph*, so wonderfully imagined and delineated by Madame Sand in her novel of Indiana, recalled to mind John Barry. He knew the sentiment which filled the heart of Margaret, and he guarded against pleading his love, which he knew could not be returned; but he continued to dwell near her, like the hero to whom we have alluded, silent, full of delicate attentions, sad, and resigned. The report of the death of Laud inspired a moment's hope, and he expressed it naturally. Margaret, who had trust in her lover, still believing him captain of a Hollandese vessel, and pursuing lawful trade, replied to Barry that she was betrothed, and that William still lived ; and our Ralph, whose lovely and engaging person, with his beautiful countenance, had not been able to vanquish Margaret's resolution and preconceived attachment, returned without complaint to his former hopeless and silent love.

In the mean time, Captain Hudson, whose identity with William Margaret did not suspect, became quite renowned along the coast. He was the bravest and most fortunate of the lieutenants of the *King of the Sea*, Captain Barwood. When the team of eight strong horses drew to the interior, armed as the custom-house train, and these cargoes of moonshine were transformed into bank-notes and guineas, it was he who directed the expedition. All sorts of manœuvres were put in requisition to deceive the coast-guard, Edward Barry, and they generally succeeded—thanks to the combined efforts of William, and the first-mate, Luff, a man of iron, whom Captain Barwood, in accordance with his habitual policy, had secretly commissioned to oversee and direct, without betraying himself, the actions of the nominal captain, and had placed him near William for this purpose. Luff feared nothing, respected nothing, and was appalled at no difficulty.

He was less a human being than a beast of prey, nourished and reared upon the ocean. William had frequently said that, when once they had made a good capture, all his desire would be to marry Margaret. The name of the young girl, whose image presided over all their exploits, wearied the ear of Luff: *"Parbleu!"* said he to his captain, "you seem much troubled. Since you will have this girl, put her on board the brig, and that will end the matter."

" Luff, I wish she should be my wife."

" Your wife she may be; there are churches in Holland and every where."

These marauders laid a plot for Margaret to meet her lover upon the borders of the Orwell, behind the large oaks of Wolverhampton-park, near the embouchure. The brig was not to be far distant, and a tender-boat was to mount with the tide to the place of rendezvous and convey Margaret to it. Luff was to personate a Dutch sailor, call at Margaret's door, and speaking a *patois*, in order better to deceive the servant, tell her to inform her mistress that her lover, who had only two hours to pass on shore, waited at the place indicated. It was eight months since Margaret had heard any thing from William, and one can imagine her joy.

John Luff knocked at the door in the midst of the celebration of one of those old Saxon festivals, which they still cling to in that part of England. Such are the *Yule-log*, ·upon the origin of which antiquarians still dispute, and *Harvest Home*, of which the name is traced back more than a thousand years. At the time of Luff's signal, the party were celebrating Harvest Home, which was united on these shores with *Hallow Largess*, that appertains exclusively to the southern part of England, and offers a singular medley of two customs of the middle age—the chivalrous cry, *largesse*, is united with the joyous clamour, *hallow*, of the Saxons. John Barry was one of the guests, and amidst the rustic gaiety, sustained by large potations of ale, his secret love for Margaret became the subject of jokes, which wounded his delicate soul. To shun them, he hastened his return to his father's house, whilst Margaret, her heart beating wildly in agitation at meeting her lover, found some pretext or occasion to quit the company, and putting on in haste her little straw hat and red shawl, without which the most humble girl in England does not think herself *respectable*, she set forth.

It was the 29th of September, 1792; for my friend Boyce, whose family were quite familiar with the Catchpoles, has marked the dates with the preciseness of a historiographer. The moon began to peer through the oaks of the priory, and the rustics were continuing their feast with great reinforcements of songs and bumpers, when two men in a little sail-boat floated with the tide to the borders of the Orwell.

They coasted along by the river-bank, seeming desirous of eluding notice, for a very singular little boat, oblong, and more like a box or coffin than a boat, followed their track; it was surmounted with floating drapery of various colours, and steered by a whimsical being, such as certes never sprung from the brain of any romancer, and of which the English in almost every sea-port offer one analogous. He was an old man, almost an idiot, who lived in this old bark, botched and rebotched, and yet full of holes; it was adorned with a sail of all colours.   His large pyramidal cap, made from his old wife's handkerchief, his long fish-hook, by the help of which he steered his fluttering bark, and the fragments of red calico, green velvet, and faded silk, which composed his harlequin sail, drew the shouts of the children and wonder of the bystanders less than did the innumerable amulets which loaded his person.   He was called Robinson, and it needed but little to make him pass as sorcerer of the sea.   He spent his life in gathering crabs and little fish, which he sold, and the old man was regarded with a sort of superstitious terror by the inhabitants of the coast.   He seemed to spy the direction of the boat, and the actions of the two men who came in it, to whom he addressed from time to time some incoherent words.

At this moment the melancholy and gentle John Barry, the Celadon of the village, past sadly over the plank thrown across the old fosse of the priory; and Margaret, with beating heart, went down towards the sea, over which the setting sun cast a roseate hue.   Her interview with William was long and impassioned—very long in the opinion of John Luff, who was quietly couched in the boat, awaiting the whistle, prelude to the seizure.

Margaret loved William with her whole soul, but he had not a stronger will than her own was in resolutions that she judged right. The resistance of the young girl whom William urged to follow him was energetic and invincible ; she alleged that it would be easy for William, become (as he pretended to her) an honest sailor, to find upon shore a situation equivalent to that he occupied on shipboard ; she did not conceal her love, but she would not yield. William thought he might gain her by acknowledging that he had not changed his course of life, that he was the famous Captain Hudson, and that she must follow or renounce him. This confession, far from triumphing over the resistance of Margaret, rendered her more determined. Then she spoke of a young man who loved her, and whose proposal she might accept if William would not renounce the smuggling business. The poor girl endeavoured by this means to draw away her beloved from his dangerous courses. But she only kindled his wrath, which increased when the name of John Barry was mentioned. After that marked combat which had left Laud weltering in his blood, the latter had felt deep hatred against Edward Barry, the brother of John.

The lovers had wandered along the bank during an hour's earnest but distressing conversation, when William, decided by the last words of the imprudent Margaret, gave the long blast of the whistle; forth issued from their concealment two

9*

men, the muscular John Luff and the old river maniac.* The last remained standing in his boat, his long fish-hook in his hand; he coasted along under the shadow of the oaks which concealed him, but his eyes were cast upon Margaret, whose hands were in those of her lover, whom she was entreating for the last time to abandon his course. This maniac seemed to possess a secret power of divination of all sad events; passions attracted him, also catastrophes; he foresaw them, he was always at the scene of action, without illwill, without rapacity, without any evil design, only as a spectator, either at a fire, shipwreck, or rapine; he said, shaking his amulets, that he saw the devil in the murderer or in the flame. Robinson Crusoe was on the spot in season this time also; for John Luff, upon a sign from William, having seized the arm of poor Margaret, she defended herself with energy against the two men, and she sent forth a piercing shriek which was said to have been heard some miles off. In the mean time, Luff carried her towards the boat, and William was endeavouring to calm her, when a new person, drawn by the clamour, issued from the thickest part of the grove and ran down to the river's side. This was John Barry, whom his comrades had banished from their festive board by their rustic jokes, and who was proceeding through

---

* The ancient fisherman, whom I have here portrayed, is not a mere creature of the imagination, but an eccentric being, once resident in the parish of Saint Clement, Ipswich, by name Thomas Colson, but better known by the appellation of Robinson Crusoe.—*Suffolk Garland.*

the park to his father's, who was forest-guard. The cry of despair reached him. He armed himself with an iron stake, planted in the sand to mark the line of the tide, and hastened to the spot where the ravishers had borne Margaret. Then commenced the unequal battle, which raged with fury between John Barry, the mate, Luff, and William Laud; the two last supplied with pistols.

William knew from the first moment the brother of the coast-guard, who pretended to the hand of his beloved; Luff knew that he must choose between taking the life of his enemy or the gibbet; more generous motives, but not less sanguinary, gave force to the blows of Barry, who had to fight against two men determined to conquer or die. Luff, stunned by one blow of Barry's stave, fell senseless; Margaret, almost as senseless, fell with him, and sliding down the sloping shore, was bathed by the rolling waves. This increased the fury of William, who, seeing Luff disabled, fell upon Barry, overthrew and disarmed him. In the mean time, old Robinson ran to the scene of action, his long fishing-hook in his hand; and Margaret, having recovered her senses, availed herself of this chance to fly from her pursuers and conceal herself in the grove, where her two ravishers could not follow her; for they had to take heed to their own safety. They made despatch in rowing to their brig, much discontented with their evening's adventure, and seeing clearly that there was no safety for them except in flight.

Barry was removed to his father's small house, afterwards to the farm of Alneshbourne, where he became the object of

Margaret's assiduous cares.   After having nursed her lover, she now became the nurse of his rival.   His wound was deep and dangerous, and Margaret viewed it as her duty to save the life of him whose life was endangered by the fury of Laud.   In her interview with her lover she had felt all that struggle between passion and duty which has been the theme of so many dramas; but she let no one know the anguish she experienced, only, as is the case with impassioned beings, she was more silent and absorbed than usual.   Her companions began to ridicule her; and those lovers whose offers she had rejected triumphed.   Barry recovered by degrees under the care of Margaret; and he alone had the generosity to defend her.   He had perilled his life to defend hers, and that augmented his love.   During this time there was a conspiracy brewing of the Barrys and their friends against William, and of the smugglers against the Barrys.   The identity of Laud and Hudson was noised abroad; he who was most positive in attesting to this fact was Robinson, whom idiotic curiosity had drawn to the affray.   William was again obliged to change his name, and he took that of Cook; a voyage to Canada, undertaken to rob the ships of the Fur Company, he thought would put his pursuers out of his track, till the remembrance of this murderous scene had died away.   Laud then became a true corsair; the inevitable consequence of crime is that it leads to more crime, and a man becomes involved, and loses the power to check his own career.

Margaret soon felt the sad effects of her union with Laud. Her friends and protectors who had aided her in her youth

withdrew; misery, hunger, and cold assailed her.   No more
was heard from Laud, whose distant cruises increased the
boldness of his course, already so violent.   One day John
Barry entered her cabin, ready to embark, and regarding
William as lost to her, he renewed his proposals for marriage.
She refused, saying she had promised her hand to another.
There was a price put upon the head of Laud : a proclamation offering a hundred guineas to whoever would deliver him
up, alive or dead, was issued.   In the mean time, the bold
corsair reappeared, and in an interview he found means to
hold with Margaret, seeing that her determination was
unshaken, and that she would never marry a smuggler, he
promised that he would engage in the marine royal service.
He executed his promise, obtained her favour, and distinguished himself.   All then went on well.   Hope was renewed
with honour, and a family of Ipswich, that of the Reverend
Richard Cobbold, taking pity on the distress of the Catchpoles, welcomed the young girl kindly to their house; and
she deserved the esteem of her protectors. .

One day young Richard Cobbold, all prepared for sport-
ing, had launched forth in a little boat belonging to his
father in pursuit of teals and wild ducks, with which these
shores abound.   The sky suddenly became overspread with
clouds, the clock struck seven, the rain fell in torrents, and
the young man had not returned; all which caused great distress in the family.   For more than a quarter of a mile, at
the confluence of the Stour and the Orwell, alluvions of mud
and sand cover the marine plants.   Nothing can be more

dangerous than this coast in time of tempest, especially for small craft. The darkness of the night and the blackness of the tempest were united. The neighbours lighted torches, hastened to the beach, called in loud tones to the young man —of whom no trace appeared. The old lunatic fisherman, who had not failed upon this occasion to be at his post, brought word that he had seen the young man coasting along by the shore in a boat a part of that day: but he shook his head like a man convinced, not only of the danger, but of the loss of the boat and the young man. Many sailors stationed at this port entreated to go in quest of Cobbold, and were ready to peril their lives in this tremendous storm, when the winds and waves seemed one. Laud, who had just returned after a happy campaign, was one of these sailors; this coast, so well known to him when he was Captain Hudson, had not a creek or shoal with which he was not familiar. He got into a long boat, armed himself with a long fishing-rod, the only implement that could aid him in feeling his way, and he steered his course slowly over the deep mud which the storm and the sea had softened. The keel of a boat buried in this mud had marked the place where the young man had disappeared; he drew him up from the bottom, unconscious, disfigured, but still living. The joy of the mother can be imagined, but not described. From this time the Cobbolds, drawn by heartfelt gratitude to Laud and his betrothed, took a deep interest in their concerns. Laud had a furlough for a few days only; it was necessary for him to leave; but he said he should claim Margaret for his own on his return, when his wages and prize-money would enable him to establish himself at Ipswich or Nacton.

During the eight months which followed this event, many sailors, charged by William with messages to his beloved, would stop at the Cobbolds; and they received a friendly greeting. But this hospitality was attended with some inconvenience : the report spread amongst the sailors that they could easily obtain a good repast with a mug of ale, provided they wore a sailor's jacket, and came in the name of William Laud. Now Mrs. Cobbold was obliged to set bounds to this maritime invasion, and for the future to suppress these aggressions upon her pantry and cellar.

Margaret had some of the erratic traits of the border life; but she was an admirable savage; an instinct of nobleness and generosity might be said to show itself in impulsive sallies; but she failed in consideration. In polished life and cultivated society there are many little inconveniences that must be remedied; if people encroach, there must be some resistance, tacit or implied ; innocent conventions which become general rules ; slight restraints for the general accommodation, which Margaret, so situated, would have readily perceived. The prolonged absence of William had had a disquieting effect upon Margaret; sometimes from weariness and sorrow she was absent, even a little capricious. This prohibition of sailors' visits afflicted her ; and in her resentment she doubtless, as is common when reason does not sit at the helm, magnified it, and acted upon it as if more stringent than the good Mrs. Cobbold intended it should be.

The next day after this injunction which distressed her so much, some one opened the door of the bleaching-yard about nine in the evening, and a little girl called out : " Margaret! a sailor wants to speak with you." Margaret, with a sharp tone, answered: " Tell the man that sailors are not admitted here, and that he must go away." Then a large packet, wrapt up in a piece of sail-cloth, fell at her feet. The large, tanned hand which, between the opening and shutting the door, had angrily hurled in the packet, was quickly withdrawn. This man was Laud himself, who had returned to bring Margaret all the money he had gained upon the sea.

She looked at the superscription upon the packet ; she could not read, but she was assailed by a secret presentiment that something portended, and she rushed out seeking to find the man; but he was out of reach. The night was dark. At the corner of the street she saw a man who appeared to be waiting for some one. She drew near, and he seized the hands of Margaret without speaking a word : this man was not Laud, but his old mate, John Luff, who, angry at the new life his captain led, and wishing to lure him back to his old habits at any price, insisted upon it that the young girl should tell him the retreat of William. A scene of violence ensued : Luff endeavoured to stifle the cries of the maiden as she struggled to free herself from the grasp of the ruffian. At length the inhabitants of the neighbouring houses ran to her relief. Then the guilty one escaped.

In the mean time, the ill reception he met with from Margaret had shaken the good resolutions of William, who believed himself forgotten. He retook his ancient courses, and despair and remorse took possession of Margaret. The report of these adventures spread throughout the county, renowned, as we have said, for its breed of horses ; and a regular band of horse-stealers, poachers, and smugglers were organized all along the coast. One of the men of William's new crew, named John Cook, coveting a most beautiful horse of Mr. Cobbold's, devised a singular means to seize him. He contrived to meet Margaret, and he read to her a pretended letter from William, in which he appointed to meet her in London at a fixed hour, and for a very brief interval. He said that " William was upon the point of starting upon another voyage. The public vehicle was too slow; and Margaret, a good horsewoman," as we have seen, " must avail herself of the bay mare of Mr. Cobbold, dressed as the groom of the stable." She did not hesitate, but in this disguise set off at a quick pace, and stopped not until she had reached the Bull Inn, in Aldgate, London, where John Cook hoped to seize his prey. But the police was already instructed; Margaret was captured, shut up in Newgate, then transferred to Bury, judged at the assizes, and, according to the cruel law of the times, condemned to death for domestic robbery. She scarcely made any defence, and listened to her sentence with submission. Owing to the influence of the Cobbold family the sentence was commuted for seven years' transportation ; but, as it was necessary to wait for the next vessel, she was incarcerated three months in the Bury prison, where, loved and respected by those who had the charge of the prisoners, she was employed in the laundry.

William, in despair, had again faced the danger, and defied the laws with more boldness than ever : at length he was arrested by the officers, and confined in the Bury prison, where he found the long-lost Margaret. The service he had rendered his country on board the ships of war was taken into consideration in William's case, and pardon was granted him. Notwithstanding the strict *régime* of the prison, he found means to inform Margaret that the next day at noon his name would be taken from the jailor's list, and could she meet him behind the church she might escape.

The long and cruel struggle of the young girl against her love had abated her force ; she had once offered up her life for William, and it would cost her little to hazard it again. She laid a plan, then, for her escape with skill and extraordinary coolness, and executed it with boldness and hardihood. The prison wall was pointed with iron spikes, and one of these spikes was broken. By means of a long cord tied to one of the spikes, she hoisted herself in the night to the top of the wall, then she slid herself to the ground outside, her hands bleeding. She met Laud as he designed, and they went to the water-side. The old friends of Laud had promised him to save Margaret, and convey them both to Holland ; but when they reached the place assigned, the boat had been so long waiting for them as to be observed, and when Laud was welcomed by his comrades, they were attacked by the coast-guard. William, twice fired upon, fell dead upon the body of Margaret, who laid senseless upon the spot, and was carried back to prison, condemned to deportation for life.

Margaret had now seen death by her side. The man upon whom she had founded all her hopes existed no longer, but she was resigned. She departed tranquilly for Botany Bay, a place of shame and exile, when she deserved consideration and fortune. The calm succeeding her only absorbing passion restored her to herself. She arrived at Fort Jackson the 20th of December, 1801. The captain of the vessel, touched by the modesty and sweetness of the young maiden, recommended her particularly to the Governor. She worked for two days in the Government *ateliers*, and then, as is the custom in penal colonies, was taken into service in a family. Colonel John Palmer, a very rich colonist, whose wife had founded an orphan asylum, desired Margaret's services, and she found her a very able workwoman. Mrs. Palmer taught her to read and write, and appointed her superintendent over her benevolent establishments. When a woman becomes interested in one of her own sex, she always desires to marry her ; Mrs. Palmer, therefore, wished to make a good match for her charge, who had never been beautiful in the true acceptation of the word, but whose vivacity now revived in her new life, free from tumult and distress. Her native grace and elegance also now shone forth undiminished. Occasions sometimes brought to light other qualities which had distinguished the heroine of the Suffolk coast. In one of the dangerous inundations common in New Wales, she saved many children from a watery grave. She herself steered the boat, and did the deed all as a natural thing, a common act. But notwithstanding her modesty and humility, she became a distinguished personage in Australia.

Margaret had briefly narrated the adventures of her life to her mistress, and her real name, supplicating her to conceal them ; and she remained in humble life, without informing herself of what passed in the colony. Even the asylum of which she was the inspectress, counted for one of its founders, unknown to her, a man who had a large concern in the adventures of her life. He was John Barry, brother of Edward, the coast-guard, and rival of Laud. He had become convinced that the deep love of Margaret for Laud would never yield. He obtained the office of inspector of the land registry in Botany Bay, and was charged with the division of land among the colonists. He sailed for Sydney towards the end of 1794, in the Bellone, frigate for transportation to the colony, where his exactitude in business, and his gentleness of character, which he always retained, ensured him success, and won him merited esteem in that country of marauders and land of punishment, where amid wild forests the corrupt civilization of Europe shows itself more reckless than at home.

The industrious and unobtrusive virtues of Barry were already crowned with honour and fortune, when he lost his younger sister, who had removed with him from England, and who took charge of his household concerns. Left alone

in his home, and wearied with the details of his large administration, he applied to Mistress Palmer to recommend to
him a faithful person to whom he could entrust the *ménage*
of his family. She recommended the condemned Margaret
Catchpole, and Mrs. Palmer then felt it to be her duty to
reveal the name of her *protégée*, and the narrative of her
life anterior to her landing at Botany Bay. J. Barry recognised his own share in the adventures, and the afflictions
of his youth were brought to mind by the recital of the
events in the life of the woman he had hopelessly loved.
His conduct was beautiful and simple. He went to the
Governor, with whom he was on terms of intimacy, and
called upon him for the complete liberation of Margaret,
and demanded that her name should be erased from the
list of the condemned. He obtained complete satisfaction in
both requests. In the interview with the poor girl, which
was contrived by Mrs. Palmer, her free pardon, which restored her to all her civil rights, was the first news he
brought, and the first word he spoke.

At the time of his wounds, when Margaret watched
over him at the farm of Alneshbourne, he had sworn to
her never to marry any other woman, and he had held to
his oath. Now the deportee received from John Barry
more than life; she was free also to accept or refuse his
offer to her, to become the partner of his life, and bear the
name of Barry. She accepted his proposals, and became
Mistress Barry, of Windsor, near the green hills of Hawkes-
bury, one of the richest estates in the New World. She

lived fifteen years in this situation, bore him two daughters and a son, and received the last sigh of John Barry, who died the 9th of·September, 1827, in her arms.   She herself expired the 10th of September, in 1841, at sixty-eight years of age, bequeathing to the Reverend Richard Cobbold, whose life Laud had saved, her letters and papers.   The Right Reverend gentleman has concocted from these a mediocre romance.   He has invented dialogues, thrust in sighs, and lavished many useless details, setting aside the real and poetical of this singular drama.   Most men let pass, without perceiving them, the elements of poetry which abound in real life.   The Reverend gentleman comprehended not the sensibility, silent and deep, of the young girl ; neither the ardour, courage, and recklessness of the young man, nor the invincible power of that passion which en-chained for weal or for woe the young lovers.   As for myself, I have visited the scenes, and been able to appre-ciate the customs and genius of the people which serves as the basis of this narrative, and I am convinced that the reality is a thousand times more interesting than the romance of the Reverend Mr. Cobbold.   In his romance of the young convict there are some ecstatic passages, joined to the most vulgar and microscopical Flemish paintings. In some pages, the Right Reverend speaks of spoons with poetical respect, of forks with mystical veneration, and descends with imperturbable seriousness to panegyrize skew-ers, tea-pots, iron spoons, washed and wiped saucepans, and gridirons, placed in their proper places.

In 1842, two men, one dressed in black, and still young, the other bearing the traces of misery which would veil itself from view, entered the museum in Ipswich. Afterwards, the youngest repaired to Kentwell-Hall, a beautiful domain in the county which he wished to purchase. He was the eldest son of Margaret. The other, whose countenance was pale, his hair thin and white, eyes keen but sad, brow furrowed, and complexion jaundiced, had met with as various and strange adventures in the chances of life as Margaret herself, whose brother he was. At the time that the connection of his sister with Laud was attended with the most notoriety in the county, this young man had disappeared— mortified, no doubt, at the obloquy that would attach to his name—departed for Hindostan, where he served with the English troops, and was distinguished by the Marquis Cornwallis. A rare suppleness of organs, and an extreme facility in learning languages and conforming to the manners and customs of the people, had caused him to be employed as a spy, and he had succeeded in many difficult enterprises. One of those chances common with Europeans who visit these countries, had connected him with the daughter of a Nabob in marriage, who soon became excited against him by some feminine jealousy, and he was forced to flee the country. Under the assumed name of Collins Jaun, he crossed the peninsula on foot, and again came to Calcutta, finding that his patron, Lord Cornwallis, had left a few days before. Then he returned to England, where, meeting the son of Margaret Catchpole, his sister, he obtained a small place from the

Government. The brother and son of Margaret, after having surveyed most of the curiosities around the museum, stopped before one a long time in silence. It was a magnificent golden pheasant, the tail of which glittered with many changeable hues, and was spread over the head in the form of a lyre. Below were these words:

" MANURA SUPERBA,
LYRA FAISAN DE BOTANY BAY.
Given by Margaret Catchpole, convicted in 1797, at Bury, of stealing a horse, condemned to death, but by commutation of the sentence, to seven years deportation. An attempt to escape caused her to be sentenced anew to deportation for life."

The son and brother of Margaret made many useless attempts to redeem this strange memorial of the condemnation and exile of their mother and sister. The directors of the museum were obstinately bent upon keeping the golden pheasant. The Museum of Ipswich still retains it ; but, thanks to Mr. Cobbold and myself, the errors of Margaret, and her afflictions, from this day, will be seen through the horizon now unknown to us, called posterity, or the future.

Such as I have described is the impression left upon two distant parts of the world of this remarkable person, whose condition was so humble. None of our most devoted heroines could have surpassed Margaret in sacrifices. This young girl had the most pure heart and the highest sense of rectitude; if she swerved from the straight line it was an error of the heart; but she committed no sin.

I love to analyze the passion of love in humble life, as in

John Barry and Margaret—a love in contrast to birth, condition, and all the environments ; over which reason has no
power ; that mysterious passion, hidden in the secrets of
God's creation, styled by the feeble a virtue, by devotees a
vice, but by the ancients a demoniacal and invincible force.

10

An Hour on board the "Swallow."

IN the chances of life, I met, in 1819, a poor creature whose adventures in their simple truth would form a pathetic romance. He was a true savage, or rather a half man. There is nothing more poetical than his life and death. I have been reproached for occupying myself so intently upon a poor half-witted Irishman. But are there not some remarkable revelations in these things? some great secrets to discover in the scarcely perceptible line which separates reason from madness, intellect from folly? Doubtless many precious subjects for observation are concealed from our view in half-savage districts where the lights of social civilization have not glimmered; and our environments in our citizen-life are not so very amusing or interesting as to obliterate the remembrance that there is any circle beyond the circle of Popilius, the narrow girdle which binds us.

It is not without a feeling of awe that I retrace here the singularly touching remembrance, which, however, may not to all eyes bear the same character. We err in judging the feelings of others by our own. Our own peculiar emotions will not suffice us in a work of art. Poet, painter, or novelist, your own sensations should be depicted simply, truthfully —that is your first duty ; but that they be in unison with other souls is also the great requisition of art.

But what I deem earnest, can it be light ? what appears to me poetic, can it be a whim ? Let the reader judge.

In crossing the British Channel during the stormy month of December, 182—, our vessel was driven by tempests into the high seas, far from her destination. The trip, ordinarily calm and rapid, was then perilous and long; instead of one day—a common passage—we passed twelve days on the ocean, and our vessel was much damaged, when a small ship of war (English) took in our crew and passengers, drawing after her the floating wreck of the little ship, her mast broken, and all her rigging despoiled.

We had on board the packet-boat an Irish priest, called Murphy O'Leary, an aged man of very respectable appearance and remarkable intelligence; a poor child was with him whose vacant smile attested that mind was lacking there. An idiot since his birth, Shillelah was now eighteen, and had not acquired a single idea: all his talent consisted in a very exact imitation of the movements he noticed ; he aided the sailors during a storm, and accompanied their nautical songs with a sort of refrain, very strange; it was the syllable *la*, twice repeated, like the lullaby of the nurse in getting her infant charge to sleep. There were various moods expressed by this monotonous refrain; it was sometimes the wail of sorrow, at others a joyful cry, and again it denoted the fearful quail

of terror. In making his prayer, (for Moran, taught by
the curate, was devout,) in climbing the mast, in dividing
the rations with the sailors, or when treated with a glass of
grog, a pinch of snuff, when chastised for his blunders or
awkwardness, it was the same refrain, varied in its intonations by the emotions felt.   Poor, half-formed being! it gave
one pain to see him—a sort of Caliban without malice, a
human body without human intelligence, a living organization without instinct.   In the evening he would sleep at the
feet of the curate, and he would sleep through the storms
and tempests, the heaving and rolling of the billows and
pitching of the vessel, without fear, without hope or foresight.

When we were in danger, Moran Shillelah conducted himself very well; the sailors loved him.   He was taken with us
on board the Swallow, where the crew were not less favourable.   At length he fell from the top of the mast, broke his
head at the hatchway, and died instantly.   The curate,
O'Leary, was very much afflicted, and the sailors wished to
bury him as one of their comrades.

Poor Moran ! I believe that many men of talent and
importance were less sincerely mourned than he.   The cabin
boys who smiled when he passed, the officers who treated him
with brandy, the old sailors who imitated his monotonous
la-la, lamented him ; but, above all, the curate, the least intolerant man that I have known.   He did not oppose the
Protestant rites at the funeral services, under condition that
he should, during the ceremony, pronounce the Latin prayers

of the Roman ritual ; for Moran had been instructed, or rather brought up, in the Catholic faith. Moran Shillelah, the imbecile child, went to heaven under the influence and protection of two different rites.

It is ordinarily in twelve hours after decease that funeral ceremonies are performed in English ships; but the tempestuous weather obliged the captain to admit of no delay. The winds whistled, night came on, dark, stormy, lugubrious. The watch-lights were placed from distance to distance, and shone in the darkness. The mainmast, illuminated even to the yard-arm, bowed under her burden—representing grief as heavy, though lighted by hope. At the tolling of the great bell, the crew assembled ; all heads were uncovered ; the rain and wind beat against their bare brows, and the rising billows laved the remains of the idiot.

Who of us has not followed a funereal train ? Who has not witnessed, even at the obsequies of the venerated and lamented, interested speculation calculating the profits and gains to the heirs ? I have followed coffins where glorious and illustrious names were emblazoned. I have witnessed pompous ceremonies, theatrical, foolish, or revolting, from the spirit of party, from hypocritical grief, or posthumous vanity. But a burial on shipboard, in the night and in a storm, was solemn indeed. Many funerals of great men take far less hold upon the feelings than did that of this miserable, feeble being. Imperfect, incomplete in physical form, this idiot was still called man, and two religious rituals were repeated over his remains, the stormy winds chanting the requiem, and a crowd of brave mariners standing with heads uncovered, not before the *ruins of death*, but before an idea —the mystery of life, above all—of death.

The winds were tempestuous, the prayer-book of the old curate was wet with the waves and rain, which fell in torrents. O'Leary murmured his solemn liturgy.

As there was no English chaplain on board, the captain read with a loud voice the service of the English Church. The great bell was still—all the sailors pressed upon deck, soaked in rain, in solemn stillness. There is for them but little space between life and death—and the sublime idea of approaching summons to eternity rolls in the waves under the keel, and peals in the blast from the mast-head. Thus the most part, notwithstanding their apparent grossness, are very religious. A thousand superstitions reign in a vessel ; the sea has her phantoms, her enchantments, her special belief. When becalmed, the sailors whistle for a breeze. As the farmer believes in the power of music, and that her charms make the bees swarm, so the officer on board believes in the power of certain magical words. Nothing could be more impressive than the attentive respect manifested by this company of sailors assembled upon deck before the dead body of the child. The captain, by the light of the ship-lantern, held before him by the boatswain, read in a clear voice these words of the Episcopal service: "Forasmuch as it has pleased Almighty God, in his wise providence, to take out of the world the soul of our dear deceased brother," &c. I heard with difficulty the words of the burial-service, so great was the raging of the tempest without, and the clattering within of cables and rigging.

The captain made a sign. An old tar, who had constituted himself the particular friend of the child, let down the corpse into the deep, which, from the weights attached to it, was soon ingulfed by the waves. All was now terminated. The stormy night gave place to a more tranquil day, and we disembarked at Ostend.

Father Murphy O'Leary, who had never visited the Continent, and who now came to receive an inheritance from a deceased relative, ecclesiastic as himself, who died in Paris, *rue des Postes*, accepted my offered services. He was a worthy and venerable priest. The day after we disembarked, he related to me the story of Moran Shillelah. I will repeat it, not perhaps in the same words as the curate, but in the exact sense of his narration.

"The mother of Moran Shillelah," said O'Leary, "lived, some years since, in the suburbs of Dublin. She tended a little stall, where she sold apples and cakes, which afforded her only support. Her husband, who had been unsuccessful in his business, died, leaving this infant child. Never was being more low in the scale of creation who bore the name of man. Moran Shillelah, as you know, thought not, scarcely spoke. Nature had sketched a rude outline, and, discontented with her success, threw it aside incomplete. His place among human intelligences was as the sheep among animals. I saw him every day seated at the feet of his poor mother, singing, or rather drawling. The school-children would torment him, and he had neither strength nor spirit to defend himself. His trust in his mother was his only human instinct. The continual swinging or balancing of his body, which you have noticed, and the insignificant repetition of the little syllable, *la-la*, was all his life and language. When the mischievous children threw stones at him, he seemed to roll himself up as a ball, and cling to his mother. Powerless to protect even his little wealth that the boys stole from him, he would utter his plaintive moan, his monotonous bleating. In the evening, when his mother returned home, her folded stall upon her head, holding Moran Shillelah by the hand, a troop of children from the suburbs would follow the idiot, who would hide his head under his mother's apron, and seek shelter in her bosom.

"The poor woman, derided by the malicious neighbours, on account of her boy, received no other appellation than the mother of the idiot. A narration of the tricks and snares to which our old woman was the victim, would be long and useless. It is true that she was ugly, infirm, and suffering, and her cries of rage against her persecutors less resembled a human voice than the hootings of the screech-owl. I had occasion to pass her almost every day. At first, the sight of this child, half animal, half human, was revolting, but it resulted in awakening my pity.

"If this flat head, forehead low and oblique, the lips pendant, the eyes prominent and vacant, scarcely expressing life, was distressing to behold, God—the powerful God, whose works are incomprehensible—had put a heart within him, and this rude and gross envelope contained a tender soul, unconscious of itself. Moran was below the brute in intelligence, above man in the power of loving. Moran knew nothing, and could not reason, but he felt that his mother was his only protector—and she was his all. She was pious. From habit of hearing her pray, he would in a measure imitate her gestures and tones. In the evening, and when the old woman went to rest for the night upon her mat in the loft, the idiot-child would kneel at the foot of his mother's humble couch, and kiss her feet whilst murmuring his inarticulate litany, a mental prayer without human words. Certainly the idea of God had not entered his narrow brain, but a species of hymn of gratitude and love exhaled from his lips. This was at the same time instinctive and mechanical. He saw God through his mother; she was the representation of religion, morality, social life, poetry, his past, present, and future. Every morning at five o'clock, when his mother would go to take her accustomed place at the stall, he would walk fearfully a little forward, reconnoitring, to see if the common enemy was in ambuscade, and as soon as he perceived an object of terror he started, pulled violently his mother's apron, and in a voice shrill and mournful sang the *la-la* which gave the alarm.

"These poor creatures, who lived for each other, moved me much ; maternal love so deep and disinterested was very touching. I found in this old woman a refutation of La

10*

Rochefoucauld : for what pleasure could Moran give his mother ? The idiot absorbed half of the gains of the poor woman, and this aged mother had to take the whole care of her unfortunate son, who could not dress or undress himself. One evening she was obliged to quit her stall a few minutes, and on returning found her boy gone. O, what despair ! She loved him for all the trouble he gave her. She at length found him on the high road, flying from a troop of little bandits, and singing his accustomed two syllables with a force which revealed his distress.

" In my daily course, I one day missed the poor woman and her child. I had given the woman some religious aid, and a few shillings from time to time, and her absence surprised me. I went to her dwelling. You, sir, have not seen a loft in the suburbs of Dublin. A person possessed of ever so little sensibility could scarcely endure such a spectacle, and I will not pain you by describing it. I found the mother dead upon her miserable bed—the child embracing her. He balanced himself as usual, singing in measure his doleful refrain, in a voice more plaintive than ever. Incapable of forming entire phrases, he had, nevertheless, sometimes the air of comprehending a part of what was said. In seeing me enter, accompanied by some persons of the house, he looked towards us with moist eyes. He raised himself, still holding firmly the hand of the dead person. His intonations were more thick and deep than usual, but he continued to repeat his *la-la*, looking at us.

" He made no resistance when removed from his mother,

but loosened his hold, and seated himself in a dark corner, on the ground.

"'What shall we do with him?' asked the owner of the house. The idiot took up a handful of dirt and covered his head, as if he wished to say to us that the earth claimed him also, and began to sing in a voice more clear, sharp, and poignant:

"'*La!* la! la! la!'

"It would have moved you to see so much affection in the poor imbecile. I had the old woman interred, and in pity I took him home with me, and *I* have never separated myself from him since, or renounced the care of the poor creature. You have seen my affliction at his death.

"For a long time I found it impossible to console Moran. A year passed, during which he repeated those monosyllables, devoid of sense, with which he had been used to wake his mother. In the evening he would look for her and weep. The ceremonies of the Catholic worship at length drew him from his grief. He imitated the gestures of the peasants, knelt with them, and his deportment at church was very proper. He hearkened to the sacred songs, inhaled the incense, lighted the candles, joined in the processions. These were all his amusements. I could not deprive him of them; it would have been barbarous. From seeing the service of mass, he learnt to acquit himself in those functions not very difficult to fulfil. In fine, he attached himself to me, his protector, as he had done to his mother. If I was ill, Moran kept at the foot of my bed; if I was absent some days, Moran would double himself up in a corner of the manse, and would eat nothing. This devotion and fidelity, like a dog towards his master, attached me to the child in spite of his incurable stupidity. He grew up before me, and I was accustomed to see him use the feeble light that nature had given in serving God through his master, and he became very dear to me.

"I was appointed to a curacy in the county of Munster. Nature there is wild and picturesque. It is a paradise of verdure. You see extended before you smiling land-scapes—rocks covered with thick mosses and decked with flowers. My mansion was by the borders of the Suir, a quarter of a league from the village of Golden, in Tipperary. A sort of grotto, embellished by the art of man, served me for habitation. You will find many abodes of this kind in Ireland; green recesses carved in a rock, half hidden by moss and foliage. If the beauty of nature, the quiet and peace of my solitude charmed me, I found in the barbarism of my flock much cause for mortification. It was impossible to discover precisely why they fought, but they fought un-ceasingly. There were some among them who had a passion for murder, without expectation of reaping any advantage from the crime. The worst elements of the human species, the mark of Cain was in them and upon them. They complained of nothing, designated no grief, but grouped themselves under different leaders, and cut each others' throats the same as they drank, played, or slept, to pass away time or enliven themselves, or as they might go to see a show. These factions, which aimed at nothing and ended in nothing, did not fail in chiefs; for wars without aim had their triumphs. Fêtes, parties of pleasure, were scenes of combat—every where was an arena, and vengeance, perpetuating itself from generation to generation, was kindling for the future new and imperishable flames. This people, who have nothing to lose but life, risk it in sport. Without country, (for Ireland is no longer a country,) without hope or possessions, they seek intense excitement, tumult, and danger. Their smothered ardour forces itself a passage. The double exasperation of political and religious hatred adds her sting to this savage violence, and these hideous tragic scenes are frequently mixed, according to the Irish mode, with giddiness and folly, even gaiety. This is the life of the peasants.

"Moran Shillelah and I lived in the midst of this savage population. I was loved; Moran was perhaps the most venerated. He never spoke. His immobility associated itself with all the ideas and images of our religion. No human passions agitated him. He was as a saint in stone, descended from his Gothic pilaster. As in the sanctuary of my church he had nothing to fear, his natural timidity and sense of feebleness had passed away. When he passed, invested in the habit of an infant chorister of the choir, which pleased him to wear, he was saluted respectfully. He responded by the sign of the cross. You, sir, can scarcely imagine the influence of Moran Shillelah. His silence, his measured chant, his presence in the church, his slow step, his eye fixed on nothing, his separation from all men; he appeared to these ignorant superstitious people an envoy from God, a superhuman being.

"I had been about six months established in my curacy; the reputation for sanctity of the young man had spread more than twenty miles around. One morning I missed him. He had quitted the house at break of day, and my search for him was useless. Three weeks passed away without any tidings. You shall hear what strange occurrence restored us to each other.

"The county of Tipperary was a prey to two bitter parties, the *caravats* and the *shanavests*, or, if you wish that I should translate these two Irish words, the *Cravats* and *Old Coats*. On both sides heroes had been hung, and immediately received apotheosis from the populace. You may ask why they were enemies. I know not; they seemed to hate by instinct. The days of fair were those in which the martial fury displayed itself specially; then my authority as parson was null. The civil and military authorities were powerless against their habits. It was the third of August, 1816, a day of fair. The heavens were resplendent in all their glory, and the beautiful valley of the Suir was charming beyond description. I left my grotto, afflicted, I acknowl-edge to you, by the absence of the child. I climbed to the summit of a hill, crowned with a fortress, the interior steps of which had withstood time. There I seated myself. My eyes followed the serpentine windings of the river, so translu-cent, deep, and so tranquil, which set in motion in her course so many mills, and without overflowing her limits, enriched

the verdant vale through which nature had appointed her
course. See, said I to myself, the true symbol of genius
and virtue; energy without violence, profoundness in calm,
and riches without excess. Engaged with such thoughts,
I cast my eyes over the village of Golden, that the Suir
crossed before she was lost in her wanderings through
fields of wheat and hops. Near the village a crowd had
assembled. The silence astonished me. Some remained
seated by the fosses on the route, others formed groups
dispersed over the field of marsh. Presently a clattering
of arms and trampling of horses met my ear. I turned,
and perceived on the left, at the foot of the hill, a detach-
ment of cavalry, accompanied by magistrates, riding, and
a battalion of infantry. It was evident that tumult was
expected, and that the civil functionaries had been warned.
I hastened down, my heart filled with fearful forebodings.
The fair was over. They hurried to conclude the buying
and selling of cattle. No person thought of overcharging
or defrauding. They folded their tents, and the peasants
returned to their homes with their cows and sheep, and
seemed impatient to leave the field free to the two parties.
Then the trumpet sounded—the troops defiled. I found
myself in the midst of the crowd. It appeared to me
that the military called out to suppress the commotion, not
having encountered any, beat their retreat much too soon.
There were many gigantic half-naked men, with heavy clubs.
Short swords and daggers were half concealed in the brown
jackets of the peasants. Every where lowered looks of

hatred and fury. I saw an old *caravat* embrace his child with tears in his eyes, and I heard curses and maledictions. Scarcely were the government soldiers a quarter of a mile off, when a great shout issued from the multitude. To this cry succeeded a fearful pause. The ranks formed. The two inimical troops, each at least 1500 men strong, who for a long time, to obey the injunctions of their curate, had deprived themselves of the pleasure of cutting each others' throats, now advanced to the valley. They brandished clubs, swords, poignards, knives, &c. A little child, dragging a sack along the ground, screamed at the top of his voice, ' Twenty pounds sterling for the head of the old *caravat!*' In less than a minute the inimical troop issued from the neighbouring thickets, and the child, who served as a herald for the troop of *caravats*, fell, struck by a stone.

"At this spectacle my blood ran cold. I flew towards the infuriated men, who I hoped would retain some religious ideas. The stones fell in showers around me. I was struck on the shoulder by an enormous one, which overthrew me; I fell between the enemies' troops. They knew me not, and my layman's dress inspired no respect in these madmen, who, for the most part, came from the neighbouring villages, and had never seen me. I was upon the point of being trampled under foot and crushed. Stunned a moment by the force of my fall, I re-opened my eyes.

"The two armies were kneeling. There issued from the bosom of the mass, not a groan or a cry, but a deep sob. It was wonderful that this remorse should overcome such a multitude.   I felt a protecting hand extended over me, and near me an unknown being, habited in a white stole, kneeling, with a crucifix in his hand, murmuring prayers.   It was the idiot, Moran Shillelah, whom I had not seen since three weeks.   He had made, with other devotees, a pilgrimage to Saint Patrick.   He returned barefoot, the pilgrim's staff tied to the end of a cane, the rosary suspended from his breast.   An enormous cross, which he took from my sacristy, was on the top of his walking-stick.

"Seeing me in the midst of the turmoil ready to perish, he came up to me fearlessly, extending his crucifix over me. No one doubted but Moran Shillelah was a celestial mediator.   All was hushed, and the troops fixed upon the idiot looks of emotion and wonder.   There were more than three thousand men in this valley, and not the slightest sound was heard.   Moran was there, who protected me. The leader of the *caravats* kissed the hem of his garment; the chief of the *shanavests* was dead.   The child, after having repeated his indistinct prayer, resumed in a tone of joyous astonishment his refrain, *la-la!*   I was carried home, and the two armies dispersed.   When I set off for France, Moran followed me."

Dear Moran! the affection of your indigent mother, your religious and simple life, your death in the midst of the ocean, your funeral obsequies upon the deck of the ship, and your sepulchre in the waves, have rendered you poetical justice to the extreme.   Poor mysterious being, seemingly half formed by his God, and separated from his kind!

Thoughts upon French Society

CHAPTER I.

RETURN TO FRANCE.

IN again returning to my native France, after my long
exile, I experienced a variety of contradictory emotions.
At first sight of France, I was affected as by the power
of magic. Paris seemed touched with the splendours of
a new creation, but a repulsive power thrilled through me,
for the decline of France was imminent. I loved her skies,
her men, her fields, her cities so gay, her conversations so
charming, held in that language replete with those exquisite
niceties and shades, that subtlety and epigrammatic point
which makes it so beautiful an instrument for expressing
the genius of the people. But I detested her want of
principle, her family divisions, and innumerable affectations.
Morals and laws at variance, words without action, action
without reason, all proclaimed the decay of vital force
and manliness.

I found that old and decrepit theories were taken for new

doctrines, foolish fancies for sense.   I foresaw the decadence of France.   As I had lost my family, and had no ties to bind me to society, I fell into deep melancholy—like a bird under the pneumatic machine, the air failed me.

But to dwell upon this painful remembrance would be to indulge in personal biography and in sentimental egotism; thereby I should fail in my resolution.   My suffering may be summed up in these few words, to adore as a mother the country you must pronounce guilty.

To pass rapidly over these wretched and solitary years, I must only say that those whom I met with after my return detested me, and that was natural, for my sadness was a criticism, my silence an insult.   My melancholy, when perceived, would scarcely gain love.   When society is in her last agonies, she would not that you should say, *You expire.*

Chance, which in England cast me among the Coleridges, Hazlitts, and Southeys, threw me, on my return to France, amidst the Jouys, the Berangers, the Benjamin Constants, the Étiennes, and all those destroyers of the old system renewed. I had elsewhere seen ardent spirits create; here their activity was occupied in destruction.   There was too much reason for this.   What they destroyed was worth nothing.   They lived in the hope to elevate over these ruins a magnanimous and splendid social system, a heaven upon earth for deified man. But that the arm vigorous to overthrow could not construct, I soon perceived.

The deep grief that the state of society and its ebullitions caused in me, between the years 1825 and 1835, could not be described or analyzed, except by means of personal details, seducing to diseased vanity—details which I have no difficulty in declining to impart. The gossip of egotism appears to me at the same time a personal weakness and a social evil. It is a fever which enfeebles the subject and infects the neighbourhood.

My life had been so grievously struck, and I was so blasted by the stroke, that I had no motive power except curiosity and the desire to comprehend those around me. In fact, I understood them, though they did not themselves. They were so much occupied with vanity, intrigue, and ambition that they mistrusted not themselves. Not one of the celebrated personages of this strange and factitious era was withdrawn from my circle of observation, and I saw some of them familiarly. In this circle there were men of very opposite opinions. My youth continued to protect me, and retain me in the sphere of a listener. How many times the ingenious author of the *Vestal*, one of the brilliant wrecks of the old Directory, wearied with my extreme indifference for an era when youth should hope all things, cried out to me, in a charming tone of sportive and kindly rebuke:

"My dear young man, you will never have a *future!*"

"Future!" When I heard him speak thus could I restrain a smile? The future, such as it proved in 1830—the future of hallucination, animated this cohort of liberals, or at least the most honest of them. It was the hope of a civilization whose near approach was a point of faith, which would be free, happy, industrial, rich, powerful; a little sensual for some, a little erudite for others—for all an apotheosis of humanity, an abstraction of God.

I heard every day a panegyric of this splendid civilization, which was to burst upon us like an aurora borealis, raying upon a rejuvenated world. These phantasms, announcing a future so ill prepared for, deluded me not. I only saw in them a prolongation of the dreams of Jean Jacques and Helvetius. The multiplied echoes of the former of these vague dreamers, which had already destroyed two thrones, had resounded a hundred times in my attentive and incredulous ears, when two fearful catastrophes, the revolution of July and the cholera threw its dark pall over the city.

How strange that our contemporaries have forgotten such warnings! They have even neglected to give a faithful picture of the scenes witnessed. The lightness and frivolity of the French is general, and causes the superficialness of their works, and also the perpetual fluctuations of opinions and principles, which keep them ever in an unsettled and harassed state. Alas! it is a nation more talented than energetic, more brilliant than profound.

The true character of the movement of July has not been designated. It was simply one of the inevitable cataracts in the wake of the great revolutionary torrent which swept us along. The popular masses were under hallucination and illusion. The leaders were not so much intriguers, or ambitious conspirators, as sceptics. They doubted of every thing, except the grandeur of man. They expected that without an absolute monarch, without priestly power, without a preponderating aristocracy, they should, by promoting the material interests of the nation and the pleasures of the people, arrange all for the best. There was their error.

After all, this new religion of material interests was only the definitive corollary of ideas which began to prevail in 1750. Neither the Spartan fanaticism of 1793, nor the voluptuous Athenianism of 1797, nor the conquering ardour of 1805 had succeeded. It remained to try the reign of interest, the construction of a society without enthusiasm, and without faith, doctrine, or love ; at the same time censorial and sensual, and armed with material resources.

CHAPTER II.

THE CHOLERA AND INSURRECTION.

I HAVE not seen in any book my night of the 28th of July. It was terrific !. The oppressive weight of the atmosphere, the pale blue of the heavens, the fearful silence, followed by great clamour, of revolted Paris—those intervals of noise and repose; now a roar of cannon, then a pause, then an irregular volley of shot from the citizens, and again silence—the heat-lightning illumining the horizon, accompanied by thunder from the Swiss guards—cries in the distance from those who were wounded by rifles fired at intervals by the wearied but still furious mob. At length the sun arose upon deserted quays, shattered columns, women upon the borders of the Seine searching for the dead bodies of their friends, and the Swiss guards seizing the first citizen passengers who passed, to avenge themselves for the night before. We have all witnessed this, but no person has reported it. Our children will only find here a record of that night—a night so tragical that St. Bartholomew, another drama played in the night upon the same shore, scarcely equalled it.

The terrible scenes of the cholera, in 1832, came to teach *our philosophers* that God was still very imperfect. Poor Paris! She was the capital of splendour and pleasure, not of resignation under the scourge, or of prudence in the lower orders, of all the most exposed to the malady. The aspect of this gay city was now appalling. The cholera absorbed it wholly; politics, the theatre, was nothing. The cholera was the end of all thought, the centre of all action. And how hideous when from the depths of Gehenna, smoking, fuming, the putrid mass issues and infects the whole horizon! The season is magnificent; the earth blooms, the heavens smile—it is the birth of Spring. In the mean time, the hissing serpent with his forked tongue issues from his covert. He is heard. All is agitation. The higher classes tremble; the urchins and blackguards in the streets begin to mock; the crowd of artisans and labourers, little used to prudence, revolt against the restraints imposed upon them. The intensity of the scourge increases. Our narrow alleys, the accumulated filth of our sewers, the story above story in the sickly and dirty parts of the city, serving for lairs for fifteen, twenty, or even thirty families; the interstices in our pavements forming so many little basins for the putrid mass of mud to exhale and diffuse itself in the sunbeams—all this multiplies the focuses of corruption and disseminates the pest. Also the mephitic noxious vapours in the dark corridors of our theatres, the stench that ascends from our restaurateurs —all the organizations of our splendid capital are deadly conductors.

But the moral malady of our nation calls for pity more than the physical. What caused me to shudder, was not so much commerce paralyzed, our theatres closed or empty, coffins carried in the arms for want of other carriage, women in mourning, the city forsaken by thirty thousand strangers in eight days, the Chamber broken up, work at a stand; but it was the sight of the ignorant and brutalized mob, mad with despair, hunger, and sedition, stopping the hearse with blasphemy, inaccessible to persuasion, defying the sanitary police, and incapable of abstinence. Who has seen these orgies of blood and death can never forget them. Alms and sacrifices were met with ingratitude and calumny.

But not to find fault without cause, is it not true that Cairo, Aleppo, Jessora, those cities of the plague, have not surpassed us in ingratitude and infatuation; that inhuman crimes are perpetrated; that the most absurd incredulity is united with foolish credulity; that the most senseless and ridiculous prescriptions for the cure, or preventions against the malady, are hearkened to even by the most learned men, whilst the ignorant and the indigent give themselves up to chimeras to which they sacrifice living victims? How often had we heard it repeated that civilization had penetrated to the lowest classes! The croakers had been so completely refuted, and convicted of calumny against our species! We had heard vauntings of the light that was diffused around, and the sovereign wisdom of the people, and a throne was demolished to prove the truth of these assertions. And here were the mighty powerless, the poor and weak ferocious, learning and wisdom confused, and the middle classes given up to prejudice and superstition. Of

11

what avail, then, your boasted progress, your philosophy, and conquests ?

Here is a people eminently civilized, a nation at the head of nations, armed with five or six hundred journals, saturated with light, and effervescing with reason. The distant lowering cloud, the murky horizon, did not appall her ; the streets in her cities so well paved, the internal administration so perfect, the industrial arts so flourishing, deadly cholera could find no access in society so organized. In the mean time the cloud descended.

Afterwards, interests set themselves in array against belief in the cholera. Political parties place the pest upon their anvil, and determine to extract something that will be useful to them. But the slime of the great city is stirred, and crime is exhaled. It is discovered, a little too late, that, in this civilization, tortured by ten revolutions in forty years, the sovereignty, after all, which constitutes the foundation and base is egotism.*

But what astonishes me is, that France should impute to her rulers the wrongs or the vices of her own doctrines which brought these chiefs to power.

---

* Here follows much upon the immorality of France, developed and brought to light by cholera.

CHAPTER III.

FRENCH CHARACTERISTICS

FRANCE, from the first germ of being, was not endowed with the calculating spirit—the *talent for affairs*, I name it. Her genius was for glory. The Celts of the ancient world were famed as brilliant adventurers. The sword, wielded by them, glittered throughout the East and West, and they were known as the most valiant of warriors. Such is the Gallic character. The Gallo-Roman, scarcely modified by twenty centuries' affiliation, under Bonaparte, pointed her sabre at the base of the pyramids. This son of the army of Brennus shook the capitol, but it trembled only for a moment. In spite of affiliations of diverse Gauls from the North and South, who are grouped by conquest around the central country, does not France remain the same? Pre-eminently social, living with others and for others, more alive to honour than fortune, to vanity than power. These are their ineffaceable elements. We became Romans as the Russians became French. What we borrowed, above all, from our masters, was not their discipline, but their elegance, their obedience, their oratory, and their poetry. Christianity afterwards diffused among us her sweet charities ;. the charm of social life was augmented. In fine. the German irruption inspired France with a taste for military prowess; but still she had a warlike garrulity, if I may so style it, easy and gay, which was evinced by the narrations of our first chroniclers and fablers. In the mean time, there was no place found for the *spirit of affairs.*

Chivalry, elsewhere serious, was with us a charming and delightful parade. At the epoch of the Crusades, our seigneurs put their châteaus in pledge, and joined in the Holy Wars. In the sixteenth century, Francis I., who spent all in beautiful costumes, had not money to pay his ransom. Under Henry IV., the counts sold their property, *and wore their estates upon their shoulders*, as said Fœneste. Under Louis XIII. we borrowed the grave courtesy of the Spaniard, his gallantry, his romantic dramas and dramatic romances. The same passion, augmented in the reign of Louis XIV., a remarkable epoch in France. Then all the ancient elements of the French character shone with intense lustre. Sociability became general, talent was honoured, the clergy civilized the people, and obtained for recompense that pontificate* of which Bossuet was first crowned. The fine arts satisfied the national vanity, and even our defects appeared a generous efflorescence, which consoled a people easy to console.

As to good financial administration, the progress of industry, the development of the business talent in France, I sought it in vain in her history. Some partial efforts and heroic starts, little supported, seemed to betray that

---

* Obtained supremacy or glory.

our nation had no aptitude for modest endeavour, and contentment with moderate success.

The financial history of France is composed of a series of mad speculations. In vain Colbert and Louis XIV. pretended to foster industry. France, in servitude, possessed not the first condition. Industry, daughter of independence, was doomed to attempt her achievements in trammels. Colbert put commerce under regulations and protecting stratagems, when the invasion of France and political events extinguished her manufactures in their cradle. During the regency, many futile attempts were made to create industry. Societies were formed; galleons were expedited to the Indies. Government was the godfather and victim to the jugglery which duped itself in duping others.

During all this time, England, her credit established, founded free corporations, under the enlightened reign of William the Third. Later, in France, the combination of riches and labour could do nothing. Voltaire, Diderot, and all the learned men, thought only of destroying the *rotten social organization*. From 1789 to 1793 their previsions were justified, and their efforts responded to. Soon followed the fourteen years of the republic—the *maximum* and the *guillotine*. Nothing of all this could create a healthy industry, but the spoliations turned to the profit of energetic men. Napoleon reigned, and he believed to sustain industry by the war which destroyed it. In depriving France of exterior resources, she was forced to resort to artificial means to supply her needs. But England,

in her struggle, maintained her resources.   The problem that
the great men of France, Berthollet, Lavoisier, &c., could
not solve in France, Watt, Arkwright, and Davy, the more
practical men in England, solved.*   During fifteen years'
obstinate struggle between the two masters of the world,
Bonaparte and Pitt, English industry fulfilled surprisingly
the difficult part assigned her.   The English army was
supplied in all her campaigns ; and when, at the return
of peace, Europe in consternation saw her losses and desolation, industrial England discovered new springs of industry,
which repaid her for her disasters.   By her, sixteen billions
were paid during the conflict—through her, all the defensive
armies in Europe received their supply of rations, wages,
arms, and munition.

English industry has for her *atelier* the globe, for her
mart the five parts of the world.   French industry, on
the contrary—a slave, uselessly active—is propped up on all
sides, defended in all parts by lines of custom-houses.   Our
warlike genius does not comprehend the business talent—it
is developed in science ; especially, the subtile science of
chemistry.   How shall those conceive great enterprises,
establish markets at a distance, associate in bold speculations, who are accustomed to the easy system of licenses ;
that is to say, permission to import or export prohibited
merchandise ?   A license creates the fortune of a commercial
house.   It is a grant for monopoly.

---

* The inventions of these extraordinary men brought so much wealth
into England that her commerce paid for her wars.

The Restoration, with some exceptions, continued this system of protection, premium, and encouragement, which agreed well with the old custom of dependencies to which the youth of France were so miserably educated.

Such are the facts that may be gathered, without much difficulty, upon the surface of our history. It is impossible not to recognise that the antecedents of France are opposed to the development of this new social phasis, called the industrial. Industry cannot result in riches of an individual or a people, excepting under certain moral conditions. Is France possessed of them?

She possesses exactly the contrary elements. France was in a chaotic state——a fusion of all ranks——no social basis, no principle, no convictions, but in a morbid state of exhaustion and weariness. There was no centre in society, no point to lean upon. Each man was his own centre, as he might and could be. Scarcely had one obtained an individuality, by riches, by credit, or fame, to be able to form a group of individualities impregnated with his principles, than, the apprenticeship served, these satellites would detach themselves, and form centres in their turn. They called that independence, but it was dissolution. There is such liberty, when the elements of the body are scattered in the tomb. From 1825 to 1840, there were every where little centres, without force, sufficient attraction, or radiation.

There had not been, since Napoleon, one centre, political, intellectual, moral, which had the least solidity——a theory that was complete, a light which was not vacillating.

CHAPTER IV.

THE DECAY OF LITERATURE.

LITERATURE, in the acceptation of the word in the eighteenth century — was it not a miserable affair ? A man would profess all that he knew not, and judge all that he took not the pains to understand! There is an age in which a man who would pass for a splendid genius, is precisely the man without a genius.   I recall to mind, *apropos* to this remark, a certain *M. de Guibert*, about whom all the *salons* in 1775 raved.   Voltaire himself wrote to him very humbly, Mademoiselle de l'Espinasse persecuted him with her love, the king sent him a snuff-box of gold.   His advent in Paris was an event, his absence left a void.   This was an infatuation without example. People called him *our* Guibert, *our* hero, *our* great man. The women were, according to custom, the mad priestesses in this reigning fanaticism.   Upon faith of the folly of the eulogiums passed upon M. de Guibert by his deluded admirers, to each of their epithets I should join an opposing one.   I would read his titles profound emptiness, cold enthusiam, absurd philosophy!

The saloons of the eighteenth century would have awarded, with a unanimous voice, a pension of forty thousand pounds to M. de Guibert, the pretender, and to the Abbé

Prévost, a man of genius, who lived unknown, nothing ; to Gilbert, a genius hated by philosophers, a mere pittance; and to Jean Jacques, embroiled with dictators of the saloons, scarcely a crust of bread !

At the present day the mania for universal knowledge destroys verdure and originality of mind.   It induces a spirit (to use an expressive word which the Germans have adopted) *discursive* and light.   A thousand reflectors, a thousand shades, as of the kaleidescope, confuse and dazzle the eye, but the great and living light is absent.   It is believed a proof of weakness to be absorbed by one idea, and to plod on manacled by that.   Thus our men will be at the same time journalists, speculators, soldiers, poets, deputies, historians, men of the saloon.   The attenuated faculties disperse themselves over all these objects to satisfy vanity, and from the thirst for glory.

Would we inquire into the cause of this unhappy decadence in literature, we must look into the past.   The constitution of ancient Europe, founded upon Christianity and war, formerly established _two great classes of powers. The illiterate bore arms, and were ignorant heroes ; the lettered were, for the most part, in the ranks of the Church. The first undertook to conquer the earth, and the second to govern it.   Their struggle constituted the dramatic interest of the Middle Age.   As the ages glided by, they bore proof that knowledge is power ; and the son of the merchant or shopkeepef, of the vassal, of the serf, availed themselves with avidity of that power which would invest them with
       11*

honours—perhaps of an abbotship, a cardinal's hat, or—who knows?—the popedom. From the followers of lighter literature—poets, romancers, dramatists, those who amused society—rays were reflected upon the mass, and honour granted to learning. The more the third estate increased in Europe, the more was learning honoured and considered a credit to it.

Unhappily, there was not in France, as in England, in the bosom of the aristocracy, a renovating power, constantly refreshing and winnowing talent and learning, and which retained it always fresh and vigorous, as in its pristine state. The failure of position for talent, the absence of allowable and just competition, was a cause the most effective and imperious of the political convulsion of 1789. Talent and the third estate obtained a place *by burglary*, as M. St. Aulaire said with much truth and spirit.

From that time the lettered ruled, and among them the boldest and most supple, that is to say, the sophists. Learning was no longer driven to seek shelter in garrets, nor did government proceed from palaces; cock-lofts ruled, and books were concocted in *boudoirs*. Many of the evils of the French Revolution proceeded from the mad reign of a literature ill understood, and classical learning ill digested.

Now the storehouse is arranged, and I see good writers and rulers, but not a *governing class* or a *lettered class*. These labels belonged to former times. At the present day, all are citizens—all may govern or print. Since the destruction of castes, education is open to all; books are circulated from the shop to the palace. The result is, that genius is shorn of her glory, pretension usurps the throne. There is no true standard of taste; regiments of light troops are formed. In a time when all would write and all would rule, and each man supremely worships himself, pretensions spring up as *fungi* in seasons of rain, but all these little thrones crumble to dust in the setting sun.

Every statesman is a learned man, and every learned man carries the ministerial portfolio in his pocket. How can the man of letters escape from political life? It is a thing impossible. If he flees to the solitudes of abstract philosophy—if he swear fealty to romance as his courtly dame, politics pursues him. Story or romance find no retreat, nor criticism an asylum. If in his story or essay any whimsical character is painted who belongs to a party, the writer is immediately classed. As all parties have absurd members, if he amuses himself indiscriminately, all parties are offended.

One of the most comical features of the age in which we live is, the great respect of the feeble and foolish for their fellows.

CHAPTER V.

REMARKS UPON THE PRESS.

THE press, in general, represents the mediocrity of intelligence. We are assured that truth, in order to be accepted, needs but to be published, which is a capital error. All the great writers, without exception, have been apart from their age — before or above it. They have frequently struggled at disadvantage. Contemporaries have fought them, and cast upon them as much obloquy as possible. Bacon, Montesquieu, Montaigne, and Locke, gave laws for the future, but were not considered as prophets or teachers in their own age. The light of reason is always odious. It is true that superiority prevails at last, but it is too late.

The press should be the gigantic mover of intellectual civilization. A noble and manly press creates a people noble and manly. It is the organ of public thought, and the condition of its existence. The activity of the press resembles echo, with her thousand resonances and spreads, while it augments the intensity of moving thought.

But if the press is free, men whom she would indoctrinate must have the power to discern. The more she extends her action, the more she demands from the reader a capacity for judgment, and an upright and vigorous understanding. It is a law in human affairs that each liberty demands a counter-poise of virtue—to each right is attached a duty. I doubt much if the French press has acquired that degree of influence to which she pretends. It is too frequently vain, venal, or factions.

How different the number of readers in France and England! All English reviewers count their subscribers by thousands ; the French by hundreds. In France the writers—fugitive and versatile, as are the readers, unstable as the country itself—rarely group themselves around a centre. Their intellectual existence is a nomadic one. They are always ready to change their banner, and even the reader is won over by a new title. There is no consistency on the one side or the other.

All respectable English families have their establishment of journals and reviews. A mutual confidence subsists between the writer and reader, and the union is sincere. All the men of the nation, writers and readers, group themselves. Thus the exercise of thought becomes concentrated—it is a national power. Thanks to this stability, to this solidity, to this grouping of faithful readers and faithful writers, the English reviews possess in England and America, and even in the East, a consideration which belongs neither to our reviews or our other literature. An article from the *Quarterly* resounds throughout Europe. If the genius of France is more liberal and brilliant, and of a wider range, the circle of readers and focus of action is not in ratio. Our talent has no central point—it is inco-

herent, ambitious, without end or aim.   Our readers send
to the libraries in quest of the popular novels, which come to
them dirty from much handling, and in their margins you
find the pencilled æsthetic remarks of the notables of the
day.   In the saloons and houses in the country they have
few books, journals, or engravings; contrary to London and
the villas in England, where these are displayed on marble
tables and ebony stands.   The recreations offered you at the
châteaux are the piano, walks, boat excursions, games; all of
them amusements for the physical: for the spirit, it may take
care of itself.

Such are our ideas and our literary morals, the worst
nourishment suffices us.   We even fear the aristocracy of
mind.   Without doubt, the aristocracy of birth, physical
power, and riches, are depraved despotisms; but, certainly,
there can be a good aristocracy.   It consists in the aspiration after the best it is possible to attain, and the perfecting
of the well-being and glory of the State.   If we had no
members enrolled in this aristocracy, where would be the
arts ? where the colossal enterprises ? how attain the great
and powerful, without their wealth and standing ? a spring
from which one can draw without exhausting the source.

We speak not now of North America, still new, and
commanded by the aristocracy of nature.   In such a country
man is still small, in the face of illimitable domains, and
unrecognised and unknown powers.   Its definitive constitution or form of government will date from its total sub-
jugation of the soil.   She has not framed her social edifice.

France has destroyed hers. All comparison between the two countries is then idle and futile. If the Americans continue the excellent education of which the English have furnished to them the elements, we can believe they may surpass their fathers. All power of action of the civilized world seems destined to be transported to them in one or two centuries.

As Europe has been decomposed, America has formed herself.

CHAPTER VI.

FRENCH LITERATURE.

THE confusion of society affects our literature. Talent is wasted or prostituted; the pretended great men surround themselves by a crowd of little men, who exalt them as sublime. The great name of author has become common and trivial, as the pavements of the streets. An excitation of the nerves is regarded as the sole end of literature. I sought for the inspiration of feeling, and found all factitious. I asked the historian for reflection and good faith, and I encountered the spirit of party. I would search for one original idea in grave prose, or one true sentiment in poetry. I wish for more nature and conscience in novels, and less attitudinizing—more sincerity in professions of faith in serious works, less bravado and showing up of vices in works of imagination. The need of the critic is forcibly felt to lay the evil spirits that issue forth tomes of popular productions, which instead of popularizing science, popularize ignorance. Compilation is more esteemed than creation, and literature is cut out with the scissors. This is an immense damage to real learning and thought.

Is it necessary to cite all the authors who have concurred in this depravation? The list would be too long.

Many of our writers have descended to the level of the bagnio, and their narrations have become matter for the Court of Assizes. The first of all beings, the man of genius or talent, is thus depraved by catering for the public, and in his turn increases the evil he should allay. Here is an enormous power dissipated. By opening the ranks to all mediocrities, as to all baseness, you dishonour the most beautiful crown of humanity.

How can we have a literature, said I, in 1830, when the critic exists no longer ? He is, to be sure, sometimes abusive and unjust, but he drives fools from the ranks, and banishes the grossest immoralities.

Madame de Staël said that Bonaparte, in becoming Consul, was appalled by the cohort of solicitors who flooded his ante-chamber. He then saw that despotism was easy to attain, and that France was his own. He availed himself of her servility : " My son wishes employment ; he supplicates for such a place." But this office is not liberty ; it is not activity, it is not labour, as far as mind is concerned. The spirit was deadened. In the barracks, many men of genius vegetated, the pen lying idle.

In the mean time, the most detestable obeisance that man can render to absolute power is to sell his soul—to become absolutely dependent. In civil business, the work executed by twenty persons, could easily have been performed by two. Keep silence, and eat your meat : at this demand thirty or forty thousand pens were agitated in France, and what was the result ? protocols, formulas of correspondence, and registers. Petrify before a table, draw a million of crowns from the coffers of the state, and return a mass of tautologies of paper. We have now only citizens, and would to God that this word was not only adopted in our language, but truly responded to in French education! Of what advantage the sovereignty of a people who are mean, superficial and effeminate? The true acceptation of citizen-rights is, the right to improvement, the facilities for progress—not for anarchy and confusion.

CHAPTER VII.

THE TRADE OF LITERATURE.

THROUGHOUT Europe we see a great fear of originality, depth, elevation, intensity; these qualities are defects in the view of those who do not comprehend grandeur. From thence proceeds diffuseness, carelessness, mixture of the turgid and commonplace, crude notions, inventions not reduced to principles, facts not verified, talents wasted or misapplied, nothing completed. To the apprehension of pedantry is mixed the love of gain; circulating libraries and reading-rooms become the rage; the writers are allotted certain dimensions; the choice little volume is under ban; there are no more emanations pure and holy, as the *Vicar of Wakefield*, *Manon Lescant, Adolphe*. There must be three volumes of a work, form and binding dictated by the taste of the public. In books of travels, three volumes with engravings; novels, three volumes cut up into numerous chapters. The necessity for engravings is another result of the material industry which has invaded the domain of talent and literature. All readers have not genius; some lack imagination, others reflection, but all have senses. Then illustrate the idea by sensible representations; bring all before the eyes; this was the inevitable consequence of the material system. If you consult the catalogues, you will find the same flood of lithographies and wood-engravings has spread over the United States, England, Germany, and France.

The Germans are behind us in these fabrications for the book trade. The novels in periodicals flourish only in France. As to the Germans, they trade in translations; they translate every thing: English novels of the lowest order, French vaudevilles of all grades;—novels, tales, every thing passes there.

True art in writing has evaporated in Europe and elsewhere; that plastic power which moulds the idea and concentrates it according to the law of supreme beauty. Precocious romances, crude translations, false historical documents, old stories varnished, valueless familiar correspondences, popular books cut and carved into manuals, concur in deteriorating real science and learning. You see sentences long drawn out, the idea is of no value. Light has quitted the summits from whence she rayed on us, and descended to the valleys, where she is diffused and lost in uncertain twilight.

Even the critic is powerless; it is the public who mark the value of the critic. When the public esteem knowledge less than show, forsake the thought for phrase; when the great condition imposed by the trade is cheap and gossiping books filled with curious matter, then the cheap and gossiping is furnished.

Does not all this warn us of the decline of Europe? above all, of the meridional part? In vain does Europe encourage a hope to the contrary; we cannot ward off the fatal truth. This decadence operates diversely according to the strength of the races. The meridional march the first. As they awoke the earliest to light and life, they will be the first to sink into the shades of night. The northern will soon follow, although the vigour and sap of the tree has not departed.

France hopes in vain through her railroads and colleges to resuscitate the vacillating flame. England herself has lost much of her Saxon energy and her puritanical ardour; in the mean time, it is in England that this deterioration is the least felt; occupied in maintaining a manly struggle against the world, the winds, the floods, enemies within and without, she entered not the domain of sophistry, that adored idol who infallibly devours her worshippers; with a great respect for talent, she has but little literature in the masses; ornaments and hyperboles, theories and the flowers of rhetoric, she has but little esteem for all that: at the moment in which we write, the farmer of Devonshire and the mariner from North-amptonshire have no desire for a child to become journalist, novelist, or barrister. England has stood firm thus far, from her belief in God and maintenance of the truth. France, on the contrary, lives in falsity, or rather dies by it. The combination of industrial trades with literature is the most adulterous alliance that can be formed; it kills genius; and, on the other hand, the endeavour to make industry romantic, destroys industry. The reciprocal effects of the commercial spirit upon literature, and the so-called literary upon commerce, is deplorable; and they equally concur in public ruin, and the falsity to truth and to themselves in our writers.

CHAPTER VIII.

TALK WITH A SOCIALIST.

I MET in Paris, on the morning of the 28th of June, near the Northern Railroad, one of my most estimable friends, at the same time the most peculiar; at least he would have passed for such at any other era. You could meet with a spirit more refined, or disposition more generous. Many slight occasions had brought to light interesting traits of character which won my love, and when I heard him develop, with that eloquence arising from conviction, his mystical and legislative theories, it seemed to me that Philo, or some old Alexandrian dreamer, had risen from the dead. In fine, he was a scholar, and an honest, intelligent man. His misfortune was in being a god. It was a sincere love of his species, without a thought reverting to self or any vanity, and he analyzed his own divinity, adored it peaceably, and communicated it to his friends. In general I distrusted these gods, and shunned them; but he, so good and true, so different from others, I loved, respected, and pitied him.

We had frequently discussed his fundamental principle, the great anti-Christian source of the errors of the age, the essential and indestructible goodness of the nature of man. I had frequently said to him that of all fanaticisms the most terrible was that which, taking the "immaculate conception of humanity for its point of departure, made her holy *à priori*, justified her follies, sanctified her evil tendencies, and deified her crimes." He replied that "humanity was to me a closed volume, that I was wrong in studying her in the enervated opulent classes, or the corrupt middle classes; that the light of intelligence had at length reached the masses, had restored to them the original grandeur and imprescriptible, or rather the sovereign, divinity of our nature; in fine, that the new baptism of the human race was to proceed from the workmen, baptism of light and fire, equity, peace, and all-embracing love; an admirable spectacle, which was already indicated by many infallible signs." When I next met this excellent man, who has not a vice nor a just idea, in the midst of the silence and consternation of Paris, he was sad, and we held together a conversation which can never be forgotten.

Every one knows what Paris was in the mornings which followed the deadly battles in the social war. You read stupour or rancour on every face; the very atmosphere was vitiated; notwithstanding the ardent glow of the sun, an exhalation seemed to ascend from the depths significant of secret hatred; and even the light of day seemed obscured by the terrific scenes around ; all soundness was gone ; moral night reigned. Where there was no glitter of bayonets, one or two passengers spoke a few words briefly and rapidly in passing, very different from the trivial loquacity of our streets generally. The philosopher and I were proceeding to the extremity of the faubourg Saint-Germain, where he dwelt, but we took the long way ; not that we were guided by curiosity, but in such momentous seasons the friends of truth feel a stern interest in searching to the depths, and endeavouring to reach the source of the evils.   All along the side of the canal Saint-Martin the streets around were deserted, and the quays were pierced with innumerable bullets, and industry commonly so rife was paralyzed.

Great silence, certain sign of the extreme of passion in the people as in an individual, which was not broken even as we approached the faubourg.   We asked information concerning our path of a shopkeeper standing at the door of his half-closed shop, the shutters of which were shattered, and he could scarcely give us an answer from his intense emotion, which choked and smothered his utterance, and overcame the national politeness.   I speak not of the houses overthrown, of the smoking rafters, of the marks of projectiles upon the walls, of entire streets unpaved, or, sight more appalling, of the wounded who were carried along upon handbarrows.   To see all the windows closed, and the gloomy visages of all the people, to hear some words scarcely exchanged in those quarters of the city where there was generally the ever-varying sounds of active industry, one may be convinced that the material disasters were not to be compared to the moral, and that souls counted more ruins than houses.   In passing through the street Saint-Jacques, and the square of the Pantheon, all that part of Paris where the struggle was most bloody, and ending at the Seine, whose bridges, usually so covered and lively, wore now the stillness of death, and the few people passing stopped not.   No more clubs in the open air at the Bridge of Arts, where the city from east to west was spread out before you, and you had the most appalling sense of the condition of Paris in seeing her closed houses, deserted and unpaved streets. We had proceeded on our long and mournful walk in almost unbroken silence, when our view embraced at once double Paris, to the left the manufacturers and labourers of the east, and the Paris to the west, that of the hotels, the palaces of the ministers; then our former conversations recurred to our minds. We entered the two camps in the midst of the city; the word *fraternity* was inscribed in large black letters upon a board which surmounted one of the gates of the Institute. *Fraternity!*

"What a libel," said I; "the *fraternity* to butcher one another!"

He replied not, and hung down his head; after a moment's silence :

"See, then," said he, sadly, "the poor armed against the rich; the famished against the glutted; despair against optimism. What are the means to appease this war? Do they exist? What think you?"

"Certainly," said I; "the material and economical fail not. That part of Paris which we have been through together, is mixed up with infectious cabins, miserable sheds, stagnant waters, paltry wrecks of houses, unhealthy workshops, interspersed with large spaces of untilled land. We have seen some houses of seven stories divided by streets two feet and a half wide, and within winding and dark staircases, without daylight or air. The labours of the Parisian ediles

12

cannot be equally divided between the east and west.   The quarter Saint-Jacques, the quarter Saint-Marceau, the quarter Popincourt, are still the stables of Augeas.   Sweep them, cleanse them.   Among the material means for ameliorating the condition of the industrial population, the purifying of these filthy streets, and the erection of convenient and large houses for labouring families, are most important; the example of London and Glasgow is before you.*   The profit of labour would be doubled, his true freedom would ennoble him, and ensure respect.   He will receive no alms, and seeing labour honoured, will feel self-respect; thus he escapes the meanness of ingratitude and envy, or the guilt and obloquy of murder. He will not quit the part of Abel for that of Cain.   He will be neither Cain nor Abel, but something better, a religious and free man.   He would not abandon a good situation unless impelled by real genius for the arts, letters, or science.

" To the operations proposed, which have already produced such good results in Denmark and Scotland, I would propose other subsidiary means, which elevate in a moral point of view, as well as a physical sense, the condition of the labouring man—baths within a few steps, or even within the house, and that the obligation to return home before midnight, and avoid all sorts of scandal, might be strictly enforced.   I would not go farther; neither should I think it expedient to open popular libraries, dispensaries, or private hospitals.   It

---

* Then follow suggestions for suitable buildings with financial considerations—no doubt most of them familiar to the public.

is well not to protect man too much; it abases him to be treated as a minor; if he feels himself free and beloved, he will be energetic, cheerful, and humane."

" I have hearkened with much interest, my friend," replied Arnaud, "and certainly, in the remedies you have proposed, there is much that is practicable and useful; but it is all super-ficial. When you have done all this, which I believe very feasible, you will not have reached the source of evils; the need of equality, and the desire for pleasures, will not be the less felt; no, the workman will not content himself with physical well-being that he is expected to enjoy. Is he not your brother ? Where is registered your right of the eldest ? Why should you guide the engine of state, and he the chariot or the plane ? The harmonies of Beethoven, are they not for him as for you ? Endowed with the same feeling, why not the same desire ? By what right do you instal him, like the Vicar of Wakefield, peaceably, mediocre, happy, in the corner of his chimney, and reserve to yourself the luxuries and epi-curism of mind and body ? This is a contrast and a juxtapo-sition which can by no means subsist."

" I love to hear you, contrary to the habits of materialists, attack the source of evil. You are right in saying that fiscal laws and economical arrangements suffice not. It is essential to change the ideas and transform the doctrines. Here is a terrible problem. To-day the evidences of the invincible brutality of these people well up before us as the floods which roll from a distant and empoisoned source. For sixty years we have been wrong-headed, even to the amount of self-destruction. In the midst of the chaos and misery that we have seen all along, and wish to remove, our philosophers and orators have preached to the people the most dissolute epicureanism. Theatres, novels, and journals have dwelt incessantly upon the ineffable beauties the poor man could enjoy had he riches. This is contending for equality in orgies, the sovereignty of epicureanism. This is not the destination of man. He must recognise elsewhere his nobility.   He is born for struggle, and by it he obtains strength and noble resignation.   This is his honour."

" You preach debasement."

" I preach ennoblement by humility ; you, degradation through pride."

" Your doctrine makes slaves."

" It forms men who recognise their limits and their rights. In what will the sovereignty of all, interpreted in the sense of each one, end ? In carnage. Mark you well, it is not to the people that I impute this folly, but to you, men of the pen. The people are the victims of the rhetoricians."

" I pass over these declamations," replied Arnaud, with perfect placidity: " I know that you are sincere, and that your severity of doctrines prevents you from being indulgent to men.   According to you—and this is the Christian theory —man is depraved. God has created him so. Thus God is the executioner of humanity. This is accommodating doctrine; by this all oppressions are justified."

" I have not said one word of that, and I do not believe one word of it."

"However that may be, (and we will return to the fundamental point,) upon the side of material remedies, you have specified some good for Paris alone. What would you recommend for moral and intellectual cures? Could you pretend to relief aside of democracy? I foresee you can do nothing without her."

"It is not democracy which has empoisoned the mind, but false principles have empoisoned democracy. Accepted as progress, she ought to elevate, not debase. It is honourable to abjure personal ambition in this chaotic and distracted season, when vanity would take the helm, and create as many masters and chimeras as there are individuals in the State. In strong nations you do not find insurgents against the teachings of experience. The Americans have hearkened religiously to Franklin, Jefferson, Washington—in these latter times, to Emerson and Channing."

"But how revive the morals and intellect?"

"Alas! nothing is more arduous. In the mean time, there is one path—education."*

"You give yourself much pains to reform man and his opinions," replied Arnaud, with supreme scorn, "as if the world was in leading-strings—as if, like a poor diseased creature, it must suffer many things of many doctors. The social war seems to you a local malady, and you call to your aid all material and moral resources as a panacea.

---

* Here follow plans for French schools and universities, and the studies to be pursued by different pupils.

The social war is quite another thing than a calamity or a delirium; it is a symptom of life and progress—a significant sign of the European crisis—an explosion little normal in appearance, and terrible as is always the explosion of great forces compressed.

"Humanity is divine. The sombre thoughts which besieged Cromwell and Pascal have for ever vanished. There is no original sin—an effete theory, calumny against God and man, and justification of all despotisms. Take notice that it is from the bosom of Calvinism, that most wearisome and violent misanthropic theory, that Rousseau and Franklin, Locke and Washington, have proclaimed the eternal liberty and natural grandeur of man. What can your attempts at reform effect against a movement so grand and vast? It is as belonging to an immense series of facts, material and moral, that the recent revolt is important. It is in that point of view sublime."

As he pronounced these last words, we arrived opposite the bridge of the Tuileries, where defiled a column of wretched men, taken prisoners during the insurrection. There were there some children of twelve years old, with defying mutinous air, lips black with powder; some workmen in frocks, young and old, dejected or fierce; some students in helmets—a sad and strange mixture of all professions, physiognomies, and costumes. The heart sinks in such a view, and public sentiment, so just and so delicate, indulges not in a remark, a cry, or even a gesture, by the side of these wrecks of civil war. I observed them a long time in silence.

"Philosopher and optimist," said I to my interlocutor, when the sad column had defiled, "while you reason with sublime subtilty upon the perfections of humanity, and upon the splendid future she is to enjoy, see the unhappy wretches who scarcely think of the explanation you give of their acts. Your doctrine moves them unconsciously.

"They reason thus: 'Since I am God, all is mine; as I am good, all that I do is good; if I am free, my actions are free.' And they follow out this reasoning. Nothing is more logical than humanity. It is false that the convicts are the majority in the insurrection that has overflowed Paris with blood. It is false that foreign gold has aided the soldiers. Venality or plunder has nothing to do with it. Your doctrine of the divinity of humanity has heaved up the pavements of our streets, and plunged our army into misery.

"Along with the frivolous, and those who are roused by clubs and the loud hurrah, alas! you see enthusiasts and fanatics, the sincere and the unhappy, workmen who are famishing, and who have left their children without bread, hoping for the power and riches you have promised them! Add to these, men of the National Ateliers, idle for want of work, and the sincere Utopian, lacerated from the evils of society, and attributing them, not to the essence of humanity, but to her riches.

"All is incomplete in this world—even the diameter of the earth has no exact measurement, and the imperfection of all things is our strength and discipline.

"In 1777, the celebrated Borda essayed to rectify, by a

special and perfect instrument, the errors of observations and nautical instruments.   He found, after all, that his invention aggravated the errors.   The instrument which he invented established the circle in ten parts, and the circle was not divisible into ten equal sections."

"And it follows from thence that we should wallow in ignorance, sluggishly resign ourselves, accept the imperfect and incomplete—submit, like the brute, to fate."

"I conclude exactly the contrary.   That which we French fail in, after so many essays, is in the worship of supreme perfection, and the feeling of our own imperfection."

We had now reached the Chamber of Representatives, guarded by pickets of the cavalry, artillery, cannons—all to protect her liberty.   The philosopher, who had long listened to my concluding harangue, as if he deeply deplored my errors, pressed my hand at parting, saying:

"Farewell, you have an honest heart."   It was as if he had said, "Poor blind man!   He is, however, estimable."   This pity of the philosopher made me smile.   Arguments, facts, terrors, evidence, all concurred to shatter the theory which was his religion, apotheosis, and worship of humanity.

CHAPTER IX.

IN 1820, at Paris, an old academician, whom methinks I see still, for he was as peculiar in person as intelligent in mind, predicted the result of the industrial spirit, (for which, by the by, the nation was becoming renowned.) He pointed out the good and evil attendant upon it. He passed for a man rather simple, and people paid more attention to his torn hat, (you all can recall it,) to his economy, his secret benefactions, to his ironical and caustic humour, and his brown coat, (eternal coat,) than to his profound and extraordinary previsions. This man was Lemontay, of the French Academy—a prophet in many things, I assure you, and who has reaped the reward of prophets. He had more ideas than words. Here is a sample of his ideas:

"The tendency to consider men as machines, to augment capital, is a formidable sign of the age. From it proceeds the grasping mercantile spirit, which invades the rights of fellow-being, and destroys faith in man. A man is valued according to his possessions. In such barbarous codes, virtues will be tariffed; the imposts will go to increase the mercantile capital ; civil war will ensue. Literature could scarcely stand in face of this livery. The fine arts would be pursued through vanity, not from taste. Sciences

12*

would be accredited, not for the grandeur of discoveries, or the sublimity of their results, but for their immediate application to some trade. Commerce would be the arbiter of honours. Politics, instead of rendering commerce honourable, would transmute all glory into commercial. At length you will see a nation where all science is concentrated in twenty heads, all capital in twenty mercantile houses, and in the masses you will see only misery, vice, and servitude, a leaven from which arises conflagration and carnage. Since finance has become a science, public and private economy will think much more of gain than the lives of men. Machines to save labour will be sought, but not to save the lives of the workmen. Have a care of introducing such hard and arid theories, which substitute the spirit of self-interest for that of fraternity, and consecrate selfish materialism, which is worse than necessity, the spring of action in the savage."

Paradoxes, cry all; petrified observations! He is behind the age! The wise old man, who thus uttered himself between 1810 and 1820, was not deceived. He leaned upon the past and the future, like all great spirits—the two points of his observation and compass. He judged not by the present, good philosopher as he was, knowing that the fugitive present never reforms itself. He was then to be seen, seeming as a book-worm, moving along the quays, with his old hat and rough old riding-habit; passing along Pont-Royal, and not by Pont-des-Arts, which was too dear; and he predicted, fifty years in advance, the Socialists' insurrection in 1848. "You degrade man," said he, "in transforming him to the working-machine, and he will make you feel it. You reduce him to the state of the polypus, where no head is to be seen, and it lives only by arms. Force, independence, capacity, you destroy—all which ennobles life—life itself. Wages will be accounted as alms, to keep the machine at work. Do you believe, then, that things can continue thus? Not so. Human nature will avenge itself. The population, brutalized by you, will be more exposed than any other to riots and commotions: for to him who has no ideas, every one presented is a novelty, and quickly works; as to one who is not in the habit of using strong liquors, a little is prompt to act upon his system. It is in the bosom of the peaceful flock that the vertigo makes the most fearful ravages. A multitude of ignorant fools rush on to blood and carnage, under the vilest of chiefs, with the blindness and impetuosity proceeding from new impressions."

Last words truly admirable, and which sums up all which has recently passed in England and France—the combats of the Socialists, their complaints, their threats their hopes, and their justifications.

We have now seen both sides of the same historical phasis, the victory and the carnage; the éclat of triumph, and the night after the triumph; a bloody night, the streets crowded with sad funerals, succeeding the victorious entrée of the thousands of pounds sterling that the ingenious barber, Richard Arkwright, and the engineer Watt trailed after them.

APPENDIX.

CHASLES, in his conclusion, speaks of the three reformers springing from the abuses of society,——Robert Owen, Saint Simon, and Charles Fourier, as proposing the best distribution of labour and wealth. He says they did not absolutely deny God and the soul, but they subordinated thought to matter; but he is far from scorning them. Their appearance typified the decadence, which was evident, of the old world. They removed some ruins, and expected to reconstruct. Of the three theories, he calls Owen's the most democratic; that of Saint Simon the grandest; and Fourier's the most poetic. But, he says, that industry the most developed, the most material well-being cannot correct the imperfections of the moral nature; Christianity and Christian virtues must lie at the foundation,——love, devotion, kindness, generosity. These systems promise him happiness only in this life; all addressed to the earthly being; and in essaying to reconstruct society, precipitate its downfall.

But Chasles, though he considers the decadence of old countries as imminent, expects Russia and America to flourish. Russia, advancing and improving from her ductile spirit, and schooled by the French; America, heir of the Anglo-Saxon genius; and behind Russia and America will arise other nations, and for many and many ages they will advance, if need be, in civilization. He despairs not of the human race and the future; and whilst kings turn bankers, literature is in its delirium or dotage, a thousand new acids are discovered, the telegraph despatching its messages by lightning, and a machine devised for killing sixty thousand men in a second, still the European world is dead or dying. In the mean time, the philosopher, from his solitary observatory, sailing over the dark and turbulent waves of the past and future, sounds the knell of nations, and in announcing the changes that are hastening on, utters his lugubrious cry: *America* is in the ascendant; Europe is no more.*

---

* A late number of the *Edinburgh Review*, speaking of the improvements in France, under Bonaparte, in roads, canals, &c.,—also the greater security and improvement of the landed estates in the provinces, which render his very name dear to the peasantry as their substantial benefactor, alludes to another cause which reconciles the French people to the present tyrant, and even keeps the name in good odour, that is the dread of anarchy and socialism ; and they condemn English incredulity in disbelieving the existence of this fear.

"Because we in the country are happily exempt from this worst of terrors,—because we have not seen our streets deluged with blood, nor our citizens decimated from behind barricades ; nor listened to the daily and hourly appeals of a depraved press to the spirit of license and murder —we quietly pronounce the whole a delusion and a bugbear, alternately got up by parliamentary majorities and successful usurpers for their own private purposes. Those who have witnessed the intermittent but inexhaustible civil war of Lyons, the bloody victory of Cavaignac, the sittings of the Luxembourg, the return by a majority of Parisian votes of men pledged to the reconstruction of society, judge a little differently : and our English views, if more dispassionate, are certainly founded on a much less familiar knowledge of the facts. Sound or not, however, it is sufficient for us that the sentiment is most deeply rooted, and that it adds peculiar strength, not only to absolute government, but especially to government sanctioned by Bonapartist recollections."

XIII.

HOME-BOOK OF THE PICTURESQUE.

A Series of splendid Illustrations of American Landscape Scenery, with papers by the most eminent writers. A new issue, at a lower price, viz.: extra gilt, $5; mor. $9.

XIV.

A BOOK FOR A CORNER.

First and Second Series. By LEIGH HUNT. 1 vol. 12mo. Cloth, 75 cents.

XV.

MARK HUNDLESTONE.

By Mrs. S. MOODIE, author of "Roughing It in the Bush."

XVI.

THE CHOICE WORKS OF THOMAS HOOD.

Comprising Prose and Verse. Poems, Whimsicalities, Hood's Own, Whims and Oddities, &c. 4 vols. 12mo. Handsomely printed. Cloth, $4.

XVII.

JAPAN, HISTORICAL AND GEOGRAPHICAL.

With an account of its present condition, &c. By CHARLES MACFARLANE, author of "British India," &c. With Illustrations. 12mo. Cloth, $1 25.

XVIII.

RECOLLECTIONS OF A NEW ENGLAND BRIDE,

AND OF A SOUTHERN MATRON. By CAROLINE GILMAN. With Engravings. Revised Edition. 12mo. Cloth, $1 25.

XIX.

FIVE YEARS IN AN ENGLISH UNIVERSITY.

By C. A. BRISTED. New and cheap Edition. 1 vol. Cloth, $1 25.

XX.

THE WORLD'S PROGRESS: A DICTIONARY OF

DATES. Edited by G. P. PUTNAM. New Edition, revised to the present date. 8vo. Cloth, $2.

XXI.

A NEW ENGLAND TALE, AND MISCELLANIES.

By CATHARINE M. SEDGWICK. Revised Edition. 12mo. Cloth, $1 25.

XXII.

COURSE OF ENGLISH READING.

Prepared for the Mercantile Library Association.

XXIII.

EOTHEN: or Traces of Travel brought Home from the East.

New Edition. 12mo., cloth, 40 cents.

XXIV.

TABLE TALK: or Books, Men, and Manners.

12mo. Cloth, 50 cents.

XXV.

HAND-BOOK OF FAMILIAR QUOTATIONS FROM

ENGLISH AUTHORS.

XXVI.

NOTABILITIES IN FRANCE AND ENGLAND.

By PHILARETE CHASLES.

XXVII.

A STORY OF LIFE ON THE ISTHMUS.

By J. W. FABENS. 12mo. Cloth, 40 cents.

XXVIII.

HANDBOOK OF UNIVERSAL GEOGRAPHY.
Edited by T. C. CALLICOTT.

XXIX.

HANDBOOK OF SCIENCE.
Edited by Professor ST. JOHN.

XXX.

TOUR OF AN AFRICAN CRUISER.
Edited by N. HAWTHORNE. New Edition.

XXXI.

A NEW WORK ON THE EAST.
By BAYARD TAYLOR.

XXXII.

ORACLES FOR YOUTH.
By Mrs. CAROLINE GILMAN. Cloth, 50 cents; Gilt extra, 75 cents.

XXXIII.

ROUGH NOTES OF A JOURNEY ACROSS THE
PAMPAS. By Sir FRANCIS HEAD.

XXXIV.

MEMOIRS OF A HUGUENOT FAMILY.
Translated and compiled from the original autobiography. By ANN MAURY. 1 vol. 12mo. Cloth, $1 25.

XXXV.

STRAY LEAVES FROM AN ARCTIC JOURNAL.
By Lieut. OSBORNE. 12mo. Cloth, 40 cents.

XXXVI.

AMERICAN HISTORICAL AND LITERARY CURI-
OSITIES. Comprising Fac-similes of Autographs and Historical documents of great interest and value. An entirely new edition, greatly improved and enlarged. Large 4to. Half-bound, $7; Large Paper mor. $15.

XXXVII.

HORSE-SHOE ROBINSON.
By J. P. KENNEDY, Author of "Swallow Barn," &c. Revised edition, with plates. Small 8vo. Cloth, $1 50.

XXXVIII.

WORKING DESIGNS FOR A WOODEN CHURCH,
PARSONAGE AND SCHOOL-HOUSE. By RICHARD UPJOHN, Architect of Trinity Church, New-York. Oblong 4to. $5.

XXXIX.

COMICAL PEOPLE ILLUSTRATED.
With sixteen Pictures, from designs by GRANDVILLE. 12mo., cloth, $1.

XL.

A FAGGOT OF FRENCH STICKS; or, Paris in 1851.
By Sir FRANCIS HEAD. New edition. 12mo. Cloth. $1; Paper, 75 cts.

XLI.

HEAD'S BUBBLES FROM THE BRUNNENS OF
NASSAU.

XLII.

———— (SIR GEO.) TRANSLATION OF APULEIUS'
METAMORPHOSIS.

XLIII.

PICTURES FROM ST. PETERSBURG.
By E. Jermann. Cloth, 40 cents.

XLIV.

THE MISERIES OF HUMAN LIFE; or, An Old Friend
Modernized.

XLV.

SICILY; A PILGRIMAGE.
By H. T. Tuckerman. 12mo. Cloth, 40 cents.

XLVI.

COMICAL CREATURES FROM WURTEMBERG.
Including the Story of Reynard the Fox. With twenty Illustrations. 12mo. Cloth,
$1.

XLVII.

A FABLE FOR CRITICS.
By J. Russell Lowell. New Edition. 12mo. 50 cents.

XLVIII.

PRAIRIE AND ROCKY MOUNTAIN LIFE; or, The
California and Oregon Trail. By Francis Parkman, Jr. Third Edition, Revised. 12mo. $1.

XLIX.

NATURAL HISTORY OF CREATION.
By T. K. Kemp.

L.

ELECTRICITY, AND THE ELECTRIC TELEGRAPH.
By Dr. G. Wilson.

LI.

EAGLE PASS; or, Life on the Mexican Border.
By Cora Montgomery. 12mo. Cloth, 40 cents.

LII.

AMABEL; or, The Law of Love.   A Romance.
By Miss E. Wormeley.

LIII.

SCENES AND THOUGHTS IN EUROPE.
First and Second Series. By G. H. Calvert. 1 vol. 12mo. $1.

LIV.

FAMILY SCRIPTURE READINGS.
By Rev. Dr. Blake.

LV.

SUPPLEMENT TO PUTNAM'S BOOK-BUYER'S
MANUAL. Being a Comprehensive Catalogue of the most Important American and
Foreign Books, published during the years 1850, '51, and '52.

LVI.

Also, a New Edition, including the Supplement of

THE BOOK-BUYER'S MANUAL.
A Guide to Formation of Libraries, &c. Comprising the Best Books in every description of Literature. 8vo. Paper cover, 25 cents; half bound, 75 cents.

Choice Books for Family Reading,

GEO. P. PUTNAM, 10 PARK PLACE

———— *Queechy.* By author of "Wide, Wide World." 2 v. $1 75.

———— *The Wide, Wide World.* By same author, 2 v., $1 50.

———— *Dollars and Cents.* Uniform with the above, $1 50.

KENNEDY. *Horse Shoe Robinson.* Revis'd ed. clo., $1 50.

———— *Swallow Barn.* 20 Illustrations, $2.

TUCKERMAN. *The Optimist.* 2d ed. 12mo., clo., 75 cts

DICKENS. *Home and Social Philosophy.* 12mo., cl., 40 cts.

———— *The World Here and There.* 12mo., cloth, 40 cts.

———— *Home Narratives.* 12mo., cloth, 40 cts.

BREMER. *Home; or, Family Cares and Joys.* Rev'd ed. $1.

———— *The Neighbors.* Uniform with above. 12mo., cloth, $1.

COOPER, MISS. *Rural Hours.* New ed. 12mo., clo., $1 25.

———— *The Shield.* (In press.)

HAYS. *Fadette, a Domestic Tale.* 2d ed. 12mo., clo., 75 cts.

IRVING. *Complete Works.* Revised ed. 15 vols., 12mo., clo.

———— *Book of the Hudson.* Plates. 12mo., cloth, 50 cts.

———— *Conquest of Florida.* 12mo., cloth, $1 25.

GOLDSMITH. *Complete Works by Prior.* 4 v. 12mo. cl. $5.

HEAD. *Faggot of French Sticks.* 4th ed. 12mo., cloth, $1.

HOOD. *Up the Rhine.* With Cuts. 2 v. 12mo., clo., 80 cts.

———— *Whimsicalities.* Ditto, do., 12mo., cloth, 40 cts.

———— *Hood's Own.* Ditto, do., 12mo., cloth, 40 cts.

———— *Prose and Verse.* 12mo., cloth, $1. Poems, 75 cts.

DESHLER. *Selections from Chaucer's Works.* 63 cts.

BERANGER. *His Lyrics.* Translated by W. Young, $1 25.

LEIGH HUNT.   A Book for a Corner.   40 cts.

———— *Imagination and Fancy.*   12mo., cloth, 62 cts.

———— *Stories from the Italian Poets.*   12mo., cloth, $1 25.

MAYO.   Romance Dust.   New ed. 12mo., cloth, 75 cts.

———— *The Berber.*   New edition.   12mo., cloth, $1 25.

———— *Kaloolah.*   New edition.   12mo., cloth, $1 25.

KIMBALL.   St. Leger ; or, the Threads of Life.   12mo., $1

LAMB.   Essays of Elia.   New ed. 12mo. cloth, $1.

———— *Specimens of the English Dramatists.*   12mo., $1 25.

MYERS.   The King of the Hurons.   12mo., cloth. $1.

———— *First of the Knickerbockers.*   12mo., cloth, 75 cts.

KEATS.   Literary Remains and Life.   By Milnes.

———— *Poetical Works.*   12mo., cloth, $1 25.

HEWITT.   Memorial of Genius and Virtue.   Illus. $3 50.

FAIRFAX.   Tasso's Jerusalem Delivered.   12mo., clo., $1 25.

SEDGWICK.   Clarence.   Author's revised ed.,12mo., $1 25.

———— *Redwood.*   Author's revised ed., 12mo, cloth., $1 25.

KIRKLAND.   Spenser and the Faery Queen.   12mo., 62 cts.

FOUQUE.   Undine, a Tale, and Sintram.   12mo., 50 cts.

GILMAN. The Sybil ; or, New Oracles from the Poets. $1 50.

GOODRICH.   Poems.   Illustrated.   12mo., cloth, $1 25.

HAWTHORNE.   Mosses from an old Manse. $1 25.

HOWITT.   Ballads and other Poems.   12mo. cloth, 75 cts

LYNCH.   Poems.   Illustrated.   New ed. 8vo., cloth, $1 50.

MONTAGU.   Selections from Taylor, Barrow, &c.   50 cts

PEACOCK.   Headlong Hall, &c.   12mo., cloth, 50 cts.

HERVEY.   Book of Christmas.   New ed. 50 cts.

COOPER.   Choice Works.   12 vols., 12mo., cloth.

CLARKE.   Shakspeare Gift Book.   Illus. 12mo., gilt. $2.

———— *Shakspeare Tales.*   Illustrated.   12mo., cloth, gilt, $2

CPSIA information can be obtained
at www.ICGtesting.com
Printed in the USA
BVHW041106150819
555975BV00017B/1593/P